THE ART OF THE SEEING EYE

Learning To Draw What You Really See

Carolyn Wing Greenlee & Stephanie C. Del Bosco

The Art of the Seeing Eye
Learning To Draw What You Really See
© Carolyn Wing Greenlee & Stephanie C. Del Bosco

First Edition
June 28, 2006

Second Edition
April 14, 2020

Text: Carolyn Wing Greenlee
Layout: Stephanie Del Bosco
Drawings & Photos by both
Front cover: Stephanie C. Del Boxco
Back cover: Carolyn Wing Greenlee
Spine: Carolyn Wing Greenlee & Dan Worley

Special thanks to Lynne Luttringer and Dan Worley who were willing to be Guinea pigs for us, even though at times it was painful and deeply distressing. And thanks to Chris Worley, my home school student, who enjoyed doing the lessons and wowed us with his sense of color.

Second Edition: ISBN 978-1-887400-59-6

Permission to copy exercise pages is granted to the purchaser of this course for the personal use of the immediate family only.
Please do not duplicate outside these parameters.
The laborer is worthy of his hire.

Rates specifically for Charter and Christian schools are available.
Please go to www.earthen.com to contact us with your needs.

Earthen Vessel Productions

Introduction

When I met Stephanie, she was eleven years old, a student at our Christian school where I was teaching art. She loved to draw, but didn't think she had any special abilities in it. In our Genesis Drawings, I asked the class members to draw something they loved. To the right is a copy of what Stephanie drew that day. It wasn't bad, but it wasn't exceptional either. That was the beginning of our friendship. We had so many good things in common: We loved God, art, and horses.

One month later we were doing drawings of negative space. Below is a copy of what Stephanie drew that day. Both of us were very surprised. She had learned how to see.

Stephanie went on to college where she majored in Graphic Design with an emphasis on drawing. After she graduated, she came to visit and ended up working for Earthen Vessel as a go-fer. We had no need for an artist, but there were lots of tasks such as applying for CIP information. Stephanie was happy to do whatever we asked, and she did it well. But then we decided to publish a book of poetry illustrated with extensive, realistic drawings. Guess who we chose to do the work? After that, Stephanie learned our computer programs and started designing our books—from layouts to covers. We had been friends before, but as teacher and student. Now we were co-workers, prayer partners, and friends. Stephanie and I had so much fun working together designing and refining this art course—which is based on the same principles which Stephanie learned when she was a little girl in my class nearly forty years ago.

All of which to say, if you love art and want to do that for a living, it is possible. Stephanie did it for years. And if you want to exercise your brain just for the experience, it will still help you think better. Whatever your interests, just remember that God designed you to be His own *poema*—His work of art—and if you let Him lead you on the path He chooses for you, there will be no end of surprises. You could end up creating something special (such as this art course) with one of your very best friends. A life lived for God is always a fulfilling and extraordinary adventure.

Carolyn Wing Greenlee

Credits

Lesson 1
Maps, graphs and photograph from *Geology*, William C. Putnam, Oxford University Press, 1964, Photograph by William Garnett, 1940

Lesson 2
Three chairs adapted from *The Art Nouveau Style*, Roberta Waddell, Editor, Dover Publications, 1977. Used by permission

Three of the chairs adapted from *Clipart & Fonts,* Macromedia FreeHand, 1984-1995, T/Maker Company. Used by permission

Lesson 3
Eagle image adapted from *Bird Cut & Use Stencils*, Ed Sibbett, Jr., Dover Publications, 1981. Used by permission

Lesson 5
Abstract painting by Joyce Van Houte, Collection of Carolyn Wing Greenlee

Lesson 6
Silhouetted tree image adapted from *Floral Ornaments-Graphic Source Clip Art,* Graphic Products Corporation, 1986. Used by permission

Lesson 7
Letters D R A W from *Ready-To-Use Decorative Letters*, Carol Belanger Grafton, Editor, Dover Publications, 1986. Used by permission; Antique car: Printers Dingbats-Graphic Source Clip Art, Graphic Products, 1989. Used by permission; Lion image: Ready-To-Use Old-Fashioned Animal Cuts, Carol Belanger Grafton, Editor, Dover Publications, 1987. Used by permission

Lesson 8
Radiolaria adapted from *Art Forms in Nature*, Ernst Haeckel, Dover Publications, 1974. Used by permission

Lesson 9
Bats: *Art Forms in Nature*, Ernst Haeckel, Dover Publications. 1974. Used by permission; Siphonophora and Dinoflagellata adapted from *Art Forms in Nature*, Ernst Haeckel. Dover Publications, 1974. Used by permission; tick, worm, fish & frogs adapted from *Ready-To-Use Old Fashioned Animal Cuts*, Carol Belanger Grafton, Editor, Dover Publications. 1987. Used by permission

Lesson 10
Linotype of Burma trees and palm tree painting: *Book of Trees*, Milford Zornes, N.A., Earthen Vessel Productions, Inc., 2004; ink painting: *Milford Zornes in Black & White*, Carolyn Wing Greenlee, Editor, Earthen Vessel Productions, Inc., 2005. Used by permission

To Milford Zornes, my teacher and friend, who shared his vision with me until I could see the truth of the matter

—Carolyn Wing Greenlee

To God, the Master Creator, and to Carolyn, my inspiring teacher and true friend, who helped me discover my love of drawing

—Stephanie C. Del Bosco

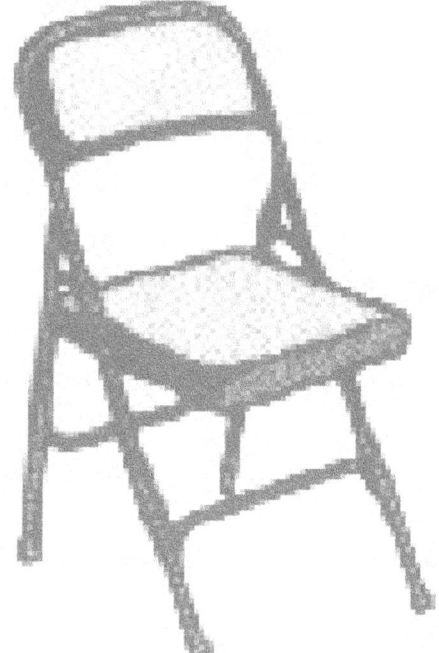

Getting Started

Welcome to this adventure into the uncharted realms of your Right Brain. There are ten lessons in this workbook, complete with explanations, examples, and exercises. Everything in this course is designed to help you develop your ability to comprehend your visual world in new and deeper ways.

You will need some equipment (listed at the start of every exercise) and a place to work. A quiet, well-lit one is best, though you can still draw even if it isn't.

Before you enter the new realm of seeing, you need a record of how you draw now.

Genesis Drawings

Please take out five sheets of paper.

1. On sheet #1, draw your favorite subject—whatever you like to draw best.

2. On sheet #2, draw a person from memory.

3. On sheet #3, draw the face on the opposite page.

4. On sheet #4, draw the chair on the opposite page.

5. On sheet #5, draw your hand.

6. Date each drawings after you've finished.

7. On the back of each sheet, evaluate your drawings. Use a scale of 1-10, with 10 being the most, and 1 being the least, rate it according to the following statements:
    A. I like this drawing.
    B. This drawing looks like the model.
    C. I am satisfied with this drawing.
    D. This drawing looks the way I wanted it to.

7. After you rate it, write your comments about it.

Thank you. Now please join our program, which is already in progress.

Attention:
Loose-leaf sheets for each Exercise are available for printing at
www.earthen.com/exercises/

Drawings of Linda Greenlee by her son, Jason Greenlee Age 18

Left: before lessons

Right: after lessons

LESSON ONE
Maintain Same Distance
Exercises 1-A, 1-B, & 1-C

neuron

If drawing were just a matter of hand-eye coordination, you'd be able to draw whatever you wanted. But you can't, or you wouldn't be taking this course. What you need to develop is not more muscles in your fingers, but more wrinkles in your brain. More specifically, in your Right Brain.

DISCLAIMER:
The original researchers thought the two halves of the brain were quite separate, each side handling its own kind of information, but now they believe it's not so much a matter of physical location, but of function. Nevertheless, to keep things simple, we will refer to them as Left and Right Brains.

Viewed from the top, your brain looks like a walnut—two halves with a connector between. As you learn things, your brain develops folds (called "convolutions") and neural pathways, which are like highways for electrical impulses to race along. The more you learn, the more convolutions you get, and the more the neurons branch out to make more highways.

If you're like most people, your Left Brain is quite well-developed. Practically everything you do stimulates it—reading, talking, adding, dividing, timing your lessons or the cookies in the oven. Unfortunately, that doesn't do a thing for your Right Brain. This course is designed to stimulated this underdeveloped and underrated part of your thinking processes. We will explain more about how that works as we go along.

Maintain Same Distance

If you were sewing a hem, routing a decorative line on a wood plaque, drawing a map of a rock formation, or striping a restored Model T, you would need to keep the distance constant. You would also be exercising your Right Brain, which loves to look at relationships between things.

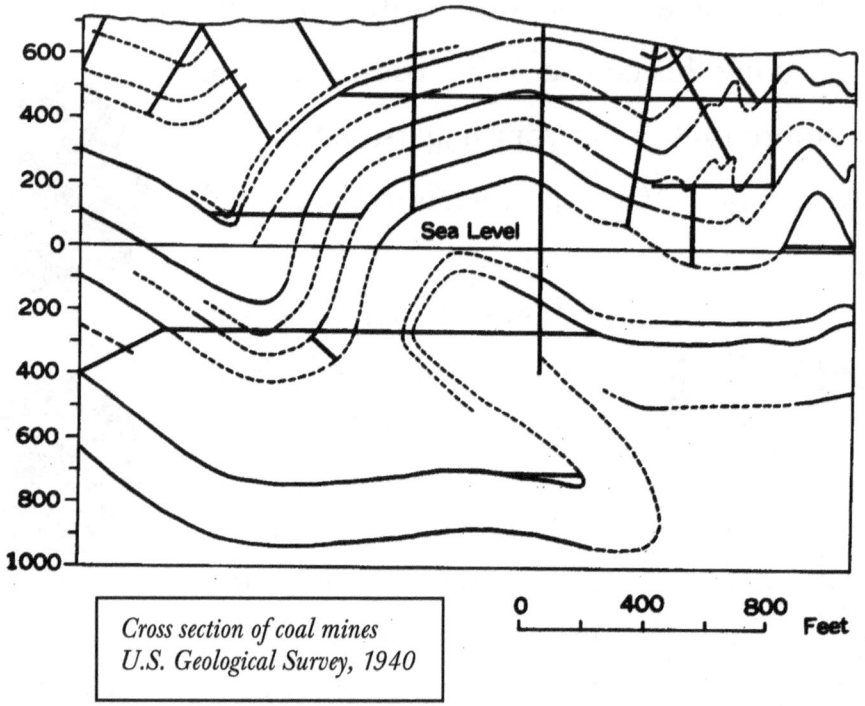

Cross section of coal mines U.S. Geological Survey, 1940

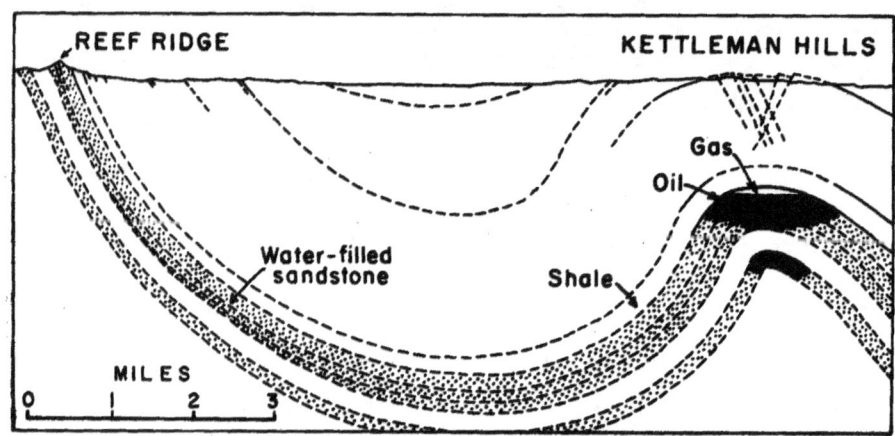

In 1943, someone drew this map of the Kettleman Oil fields for the California State Division of Mines

Instruction:

SUPPLIES NEEDED:

1. Quiet, well-lit place to work
2. Pencil
3. Colored Pencils (Blue & Green)
4. Sharpener

Exercise 1-A

Please take out your first exercise, sheet 1-A. You will see three lines, each with two dots at each end—one above and one below. Your job is to create a line above and one below the original, maintaining the same distance as the dot so that you end up on the dots at other end. You may go either direction—left to right or right to left.

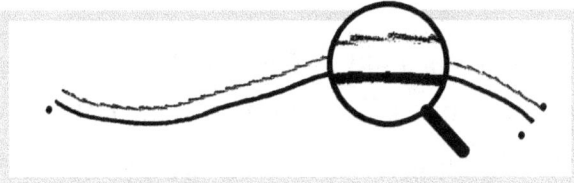

The best way to accomplish this task is to use small, short strokes with a pencil—use a light, feathery touch. If you try to keep the distance correct without lifting the pencil you might feel as if you're driving a shopping cart with a bad wheel. You'll find yourself veering off-course and out of control. So lift the pencil off the paper frequently. That allows you to correct your course before it gets too far off. If you start to get off, don't erase; go back to where you began to veer and resume from there at the proper distance. Take your time. This is not a race. Neither is it an English composition. Feel free to turn the paper as you navigate the curves, adjusting it to whatever is comfortable to you.

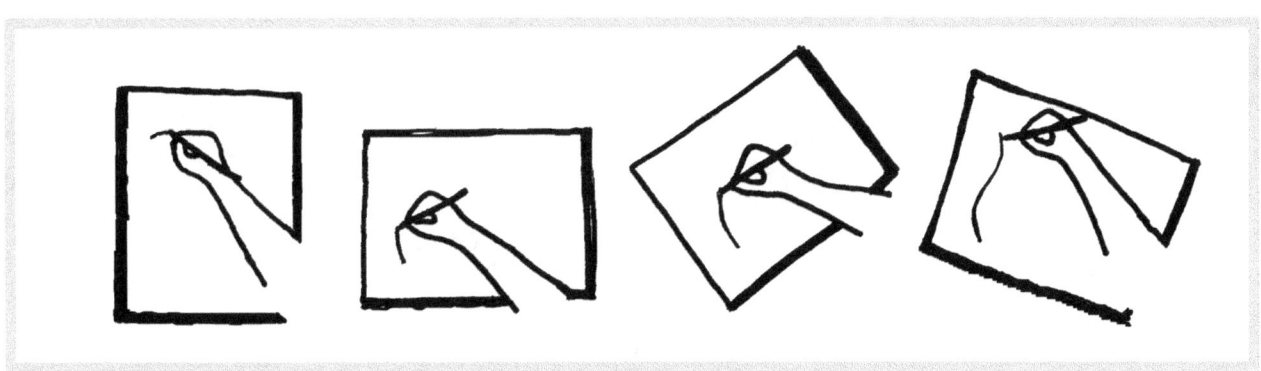

Maintain Same Distance • Lesson 1

When you've finished all six lines on 1-A, go back and look at the first set of lines. With a green pencil, circle the areas where you see there's too much space (it may bulge like a boa constrictor that's swallowed a cow). With a blue pencil, circle those areas where there is too little space. Don't feel bad if your first set looks like a beaded necklace. Learning to evaluate your own work is one of the most important things an artist can do.

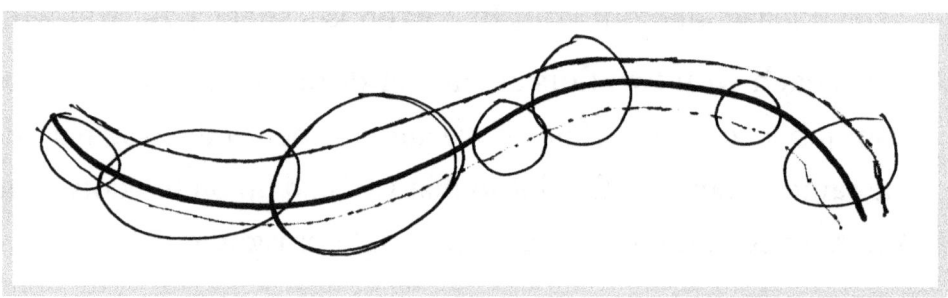

Exercise 1-B

On Sheet A-2, repeat this process from page 1, maintaining the same distance from each of the next three lines. Take your time. There's no hurry. Your Right Brain loves this. If you lose track of time, it's because your Right Brain is fully engaged. Then, when you're finished, evaluate as before. Were you more consistent this time?

Are you tired? Some people think this lesson is really easy and fun. Some people think it's pure torture. My friend Lynne is one of those. A person who is a whiz at balancing checkbooks and proofreading manuscripts, but not someone who considers herself gifted in the arts, she reluctantly agreed to help us evaluate this art course by completing all the lessons. She hated this first exercise. Look below to see how she did.

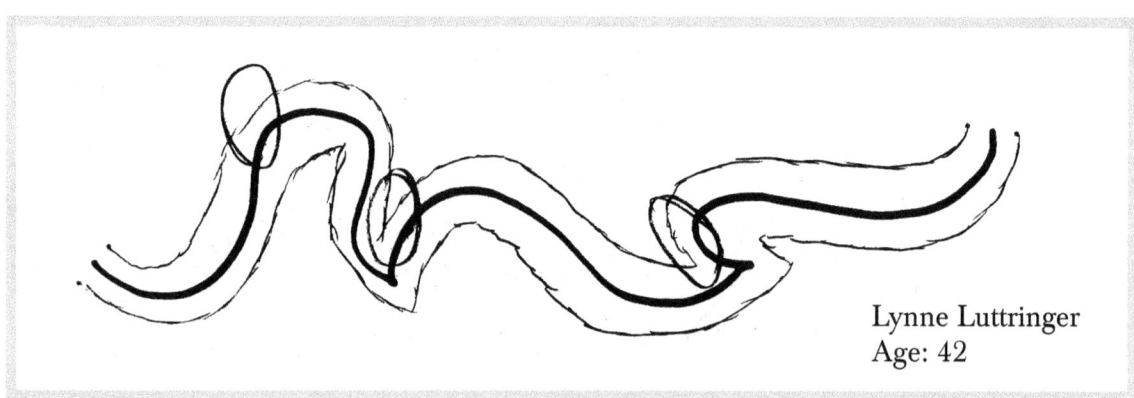

Lynne Luttringer
Age: 42

Why was it so hard for Lynne? Her Left Brain is amply developed; her Right Brain is not. You know what happens when you start to exercise flabby muscles? You get tired. You get sore. You might get irritated. Lynne even got hostile. If any of that happens to you, don't worry. Developing your Right Brain this way is a lot of work. That's why we call it "exercise."

Exercise 1-C

Before tackling the last exercise, take a stretch, get up and move around a bit. Then choose one of the sheets numbered 1-C, either the parakeet, fish, or sailboat. Starting at the dot within the object, draw your line, maintaining the same distance from the original outline all the way around till you meet the end of your new line. Then draw another line, maintaining the same distance from the one you just drew. Repeat this process until the entire space is filled. When you're done, color your creation. If you cut it out and paste it on colored paper, it would make a respectable greeting card. If you would like to do any of the others, feel free.

If you were a geologist, a modern artist, or a fabric designer, you might want to copy the pattern of this thinly bedded clayey limestone photographed by William Garnett in the 1940s.

Maintain Same Distance • Lesson 1

Attention:

Loose-leaf sheets for each Exercise are available for printing at www.earthen.com/exercises/

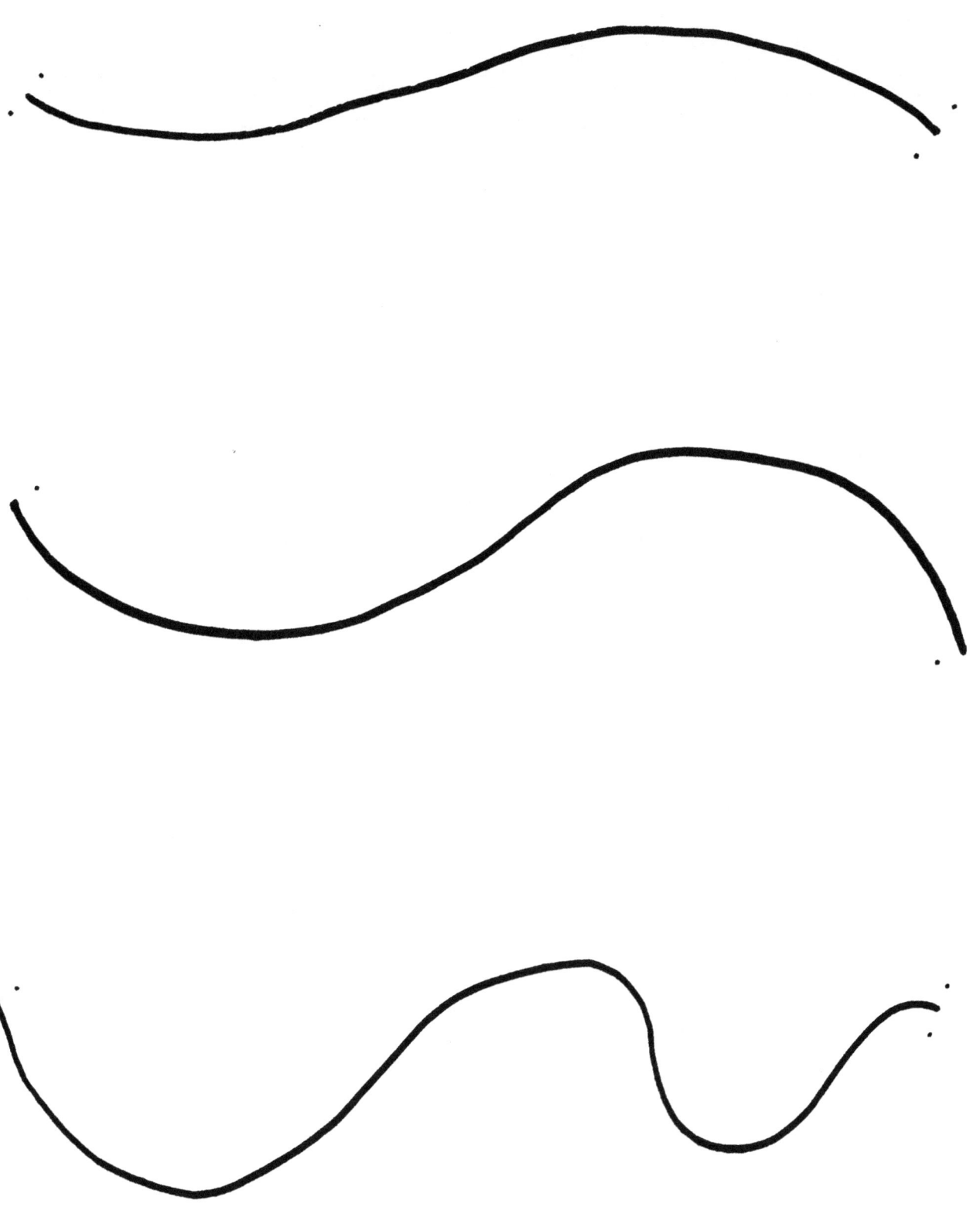

Maintain Same Distance • Lesson 1 • Exercise 1-A

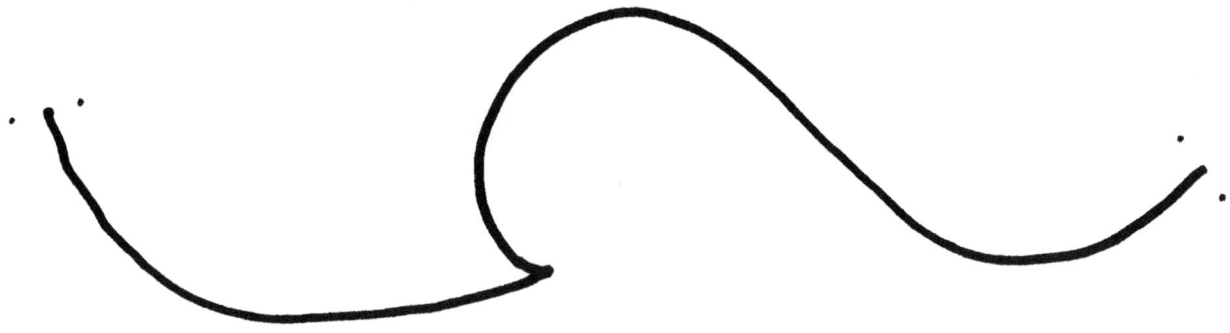
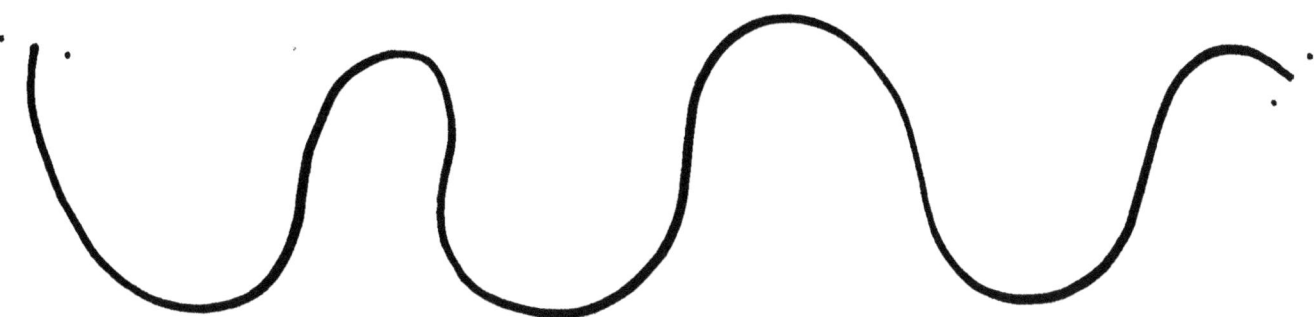
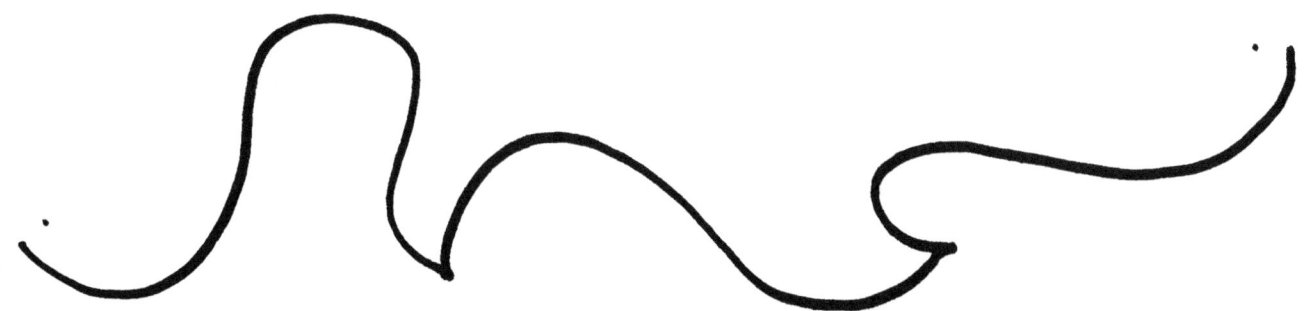

Maintain Same Distance • Lesson 1 • Exercise 1-B

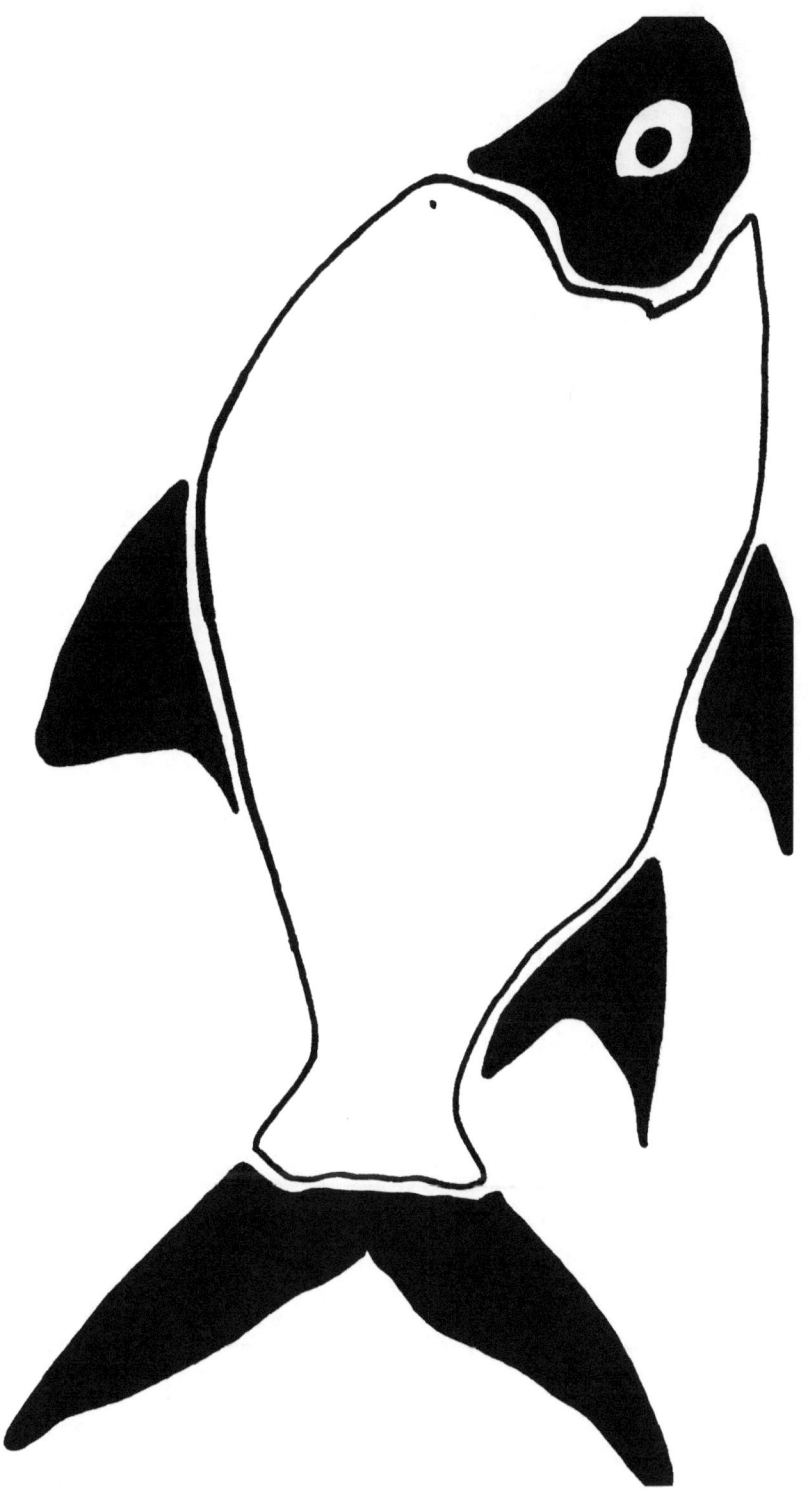

Maintain Same Distance • Lesson 1 • Exercise 1-C

LESSON TWO

Squares of Different Patterns
Exercise 2-A

Someone said if you can write your name, you can draw. But, as we said at the beginning, you may have the hand-eye coordination, but your drawings still don't look the way you want. What's missing?

What's missing is the Seeing. The Left Brain tends to rapidly identify and be satisfied— "I see, it's a chair. Now leave me alone." The Right Brain is not concerned with labels. It likes to revel in the details, enjoying the relationships of space and line, textures, nuances, colors, shapes. The Left Brain knows that a chair usually has four legs of equal length and a seat that's level with the floor. But the Right Brain sees that two legs appear to be shorter than the other two and the seat which is wide and deep enough to accommodate most bottoms looks like a hot dog. Therefore, the Left Brain will bring forth a picture that may look like this whereas the Right Brain will make a drawing this.

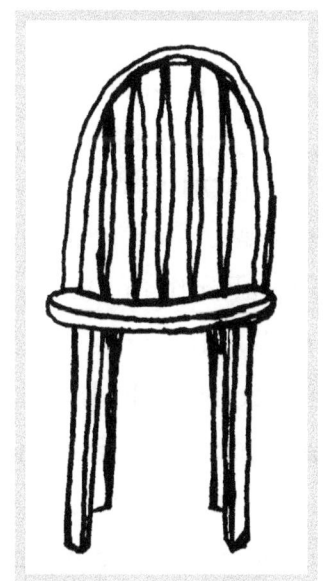

You are riding in a car. There are two people in the car ahead of you. How big are the heads inside the other car?

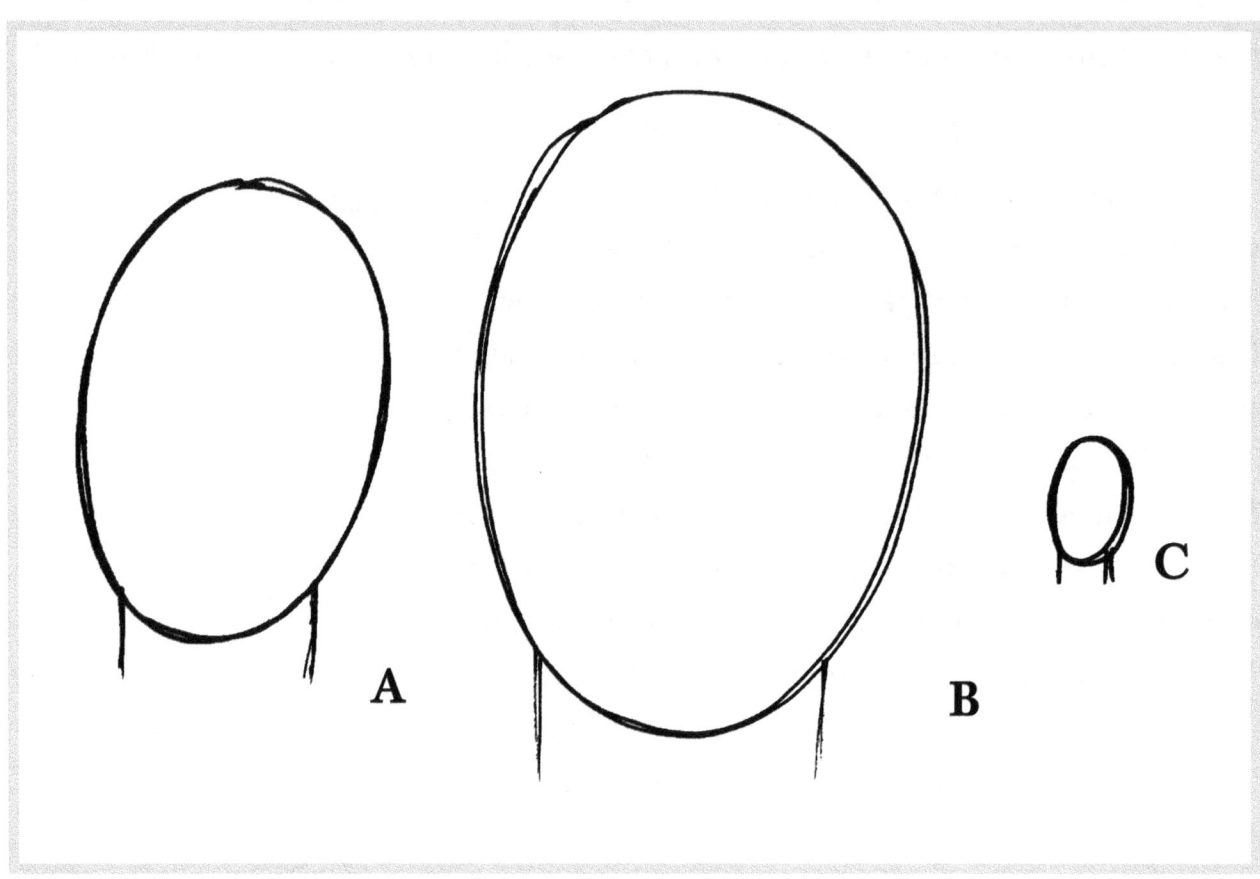

Choose an answer (A, B, or C): _____

The answer to the question is C. Surprised?

Next time you drive, check it out. Measure with your thumb the sizes of the heads in other cars. They look much smaller than you would suppose. That's because your Left Brain knows that they are really about the same size as your head and the heads of your family, friends, and pets. Your Right Brain, on the other side, sees what it really LOOKS like—not the correct measurement in inches, but the proportion according to distance and perspective.

This next section will help you see what's really there. But first a few definitions.

PARALLEL

PARALLEL means that the lines are the same distance apart. Railroad tracks are a good example. So are the rungs of a ladder.

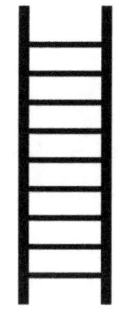

perpendicular

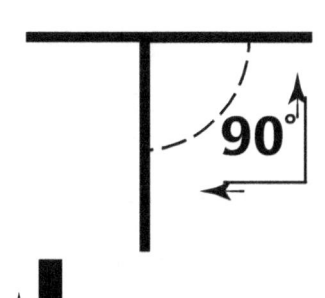

The ties of the railroad track are not parallel to the track. They are PERPENDICULAR. That means that they are at right angles (90°) to each other. The letters "H" and "T" have cross pieces that are perpendicular to the vertical lines.

VERTICAL

VERTICAL means that they go up and down, not sideways. People stand up vertically (mostly). The letter "I" is vertical. The long part of the capital letter "L" is vertical. It also has a shorter part which is perpendicular to the vertical part. That shorter part is horizontal.

horizontal

HORIZONTAL means side to side. The horizon is a good example. The letter "E" has three horizontal lines. How many vertical ones does it have?

_____

DIAGONAL

DIAGONAL means slanting. The letter "Z" has a diagonal line. What are the other two lines?

_____ & _____

Squares of Different Patterns • Lesson 2   **19**

PRACTICE

Draw a diagonal line:	Draw a vertical line:	Draw a horizontal line:
Draw two parallel lines:	Draw a line that is perpendicular to another:	

base line

One more time. When we say "base line," we mean a horizontal line that you draw touching the bottom of the image.

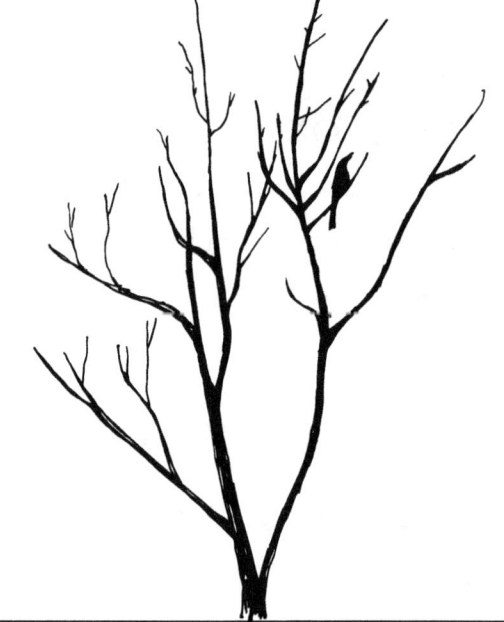

MEASURING

All the measuring you will be doing in this course will be done with the pencil held as close to flat against the paper as possible. Use the eraser-end of your pencil when measuring.

A way to measure horizontals:

1. Hold the measuring pencil in the hand with which you do not draw.

2. Put the end of the eraser at point "A".

3. Keeping the pencil horizontal, put your thumbnail on the pencil at the place where the base line ends (on the left if you're measuring with your left hand, on the right if you're measuring with your right).

4. Without moving your thumbnail, move your measuring pencil to Base Line X.

5. Position your thumbnail at the base line.

6. With the pencil in your drawing hand, put a light pencil line at the end of the eraser.

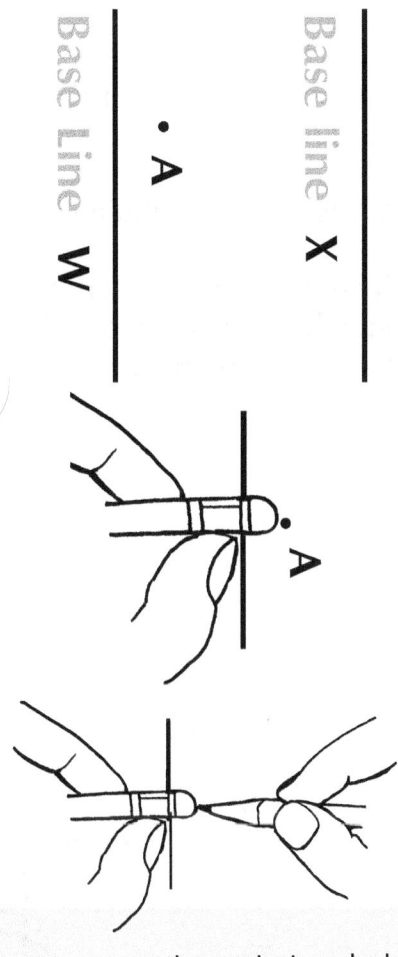

Have you ever seen artists painting, holding their brushes up vertically and squinting at the subject with one eye? They're measuring with the brush handle and their thumb This is the source of the expression "Rule of Thumb."

Squares of Different Patterns • Lesson 2   **21**

A way to measure verticals:

1. Hold the measuring pencil in the hand with which you do not draw.

2. Put the end of the eraser at point A.

3. Put your thumbnail on the pencil at the place it crosses Base Line Y.

4. Without moving your thumb nail, move your measuring pencil to Base Line Z.

5. Position your thumb nail at the base line.

6. Keeping the pencil vertical in your drawing hand, put a light pencil line at the end of the eraser of the measuring pencil.

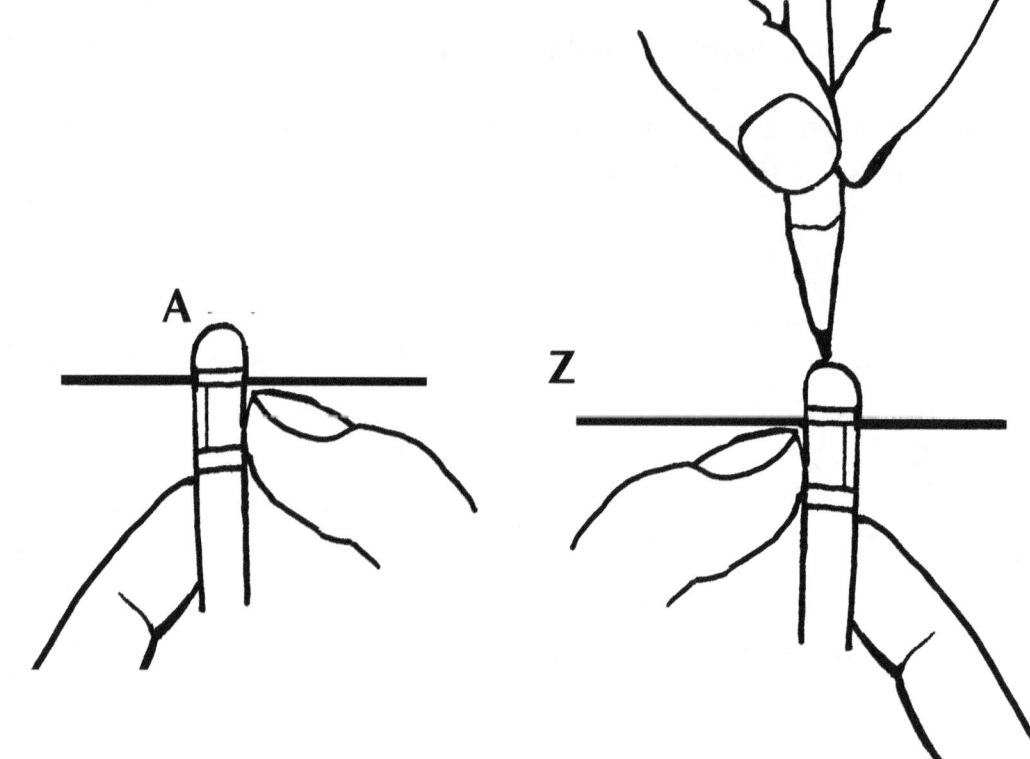

Instruction:

SUPPLIES NEEDED:

1. Quiet, well-lit place to work
2. Pencil
3. Eraser
4. Colored pencils
5. Sharpener
6. Black, small-tipped marking pen

Exercise 2-A

Half of the boxes on Sheet 2-A have squiggly lines. Half are empty. In the empty boxes duplicate the lines and spaces that are in the decorated ones. Feel free to rotate your paper.

To get an accurate starting point for your first line, measure with your pencil the distance from the base line of the box to the place where it contacts the line. Put your thumbnail on the pencil at the level of the contact.

Using your measurement, make a mark on the empty box. Then, with short, light, feathery strokes, begin to copy the line, maintaining the relationships of curve and space that you see in the original. If you get lost, simply measure again and adjust accordingly.

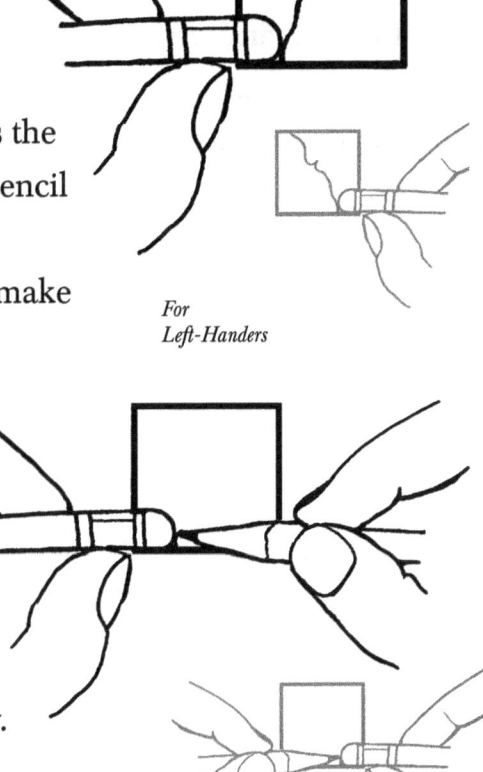

For Left-Handers

Squares of Different Patterns • Lesson 2

Evaluate your work. Erase and fix whatever is inaccurate.

> ## Evaluate:
> 1. Are the curves and spaces accurate?
> 2. Do the boxes look like the original?
>   How are the shapes different?

When you are satisfied that your pencil lines are fairly accurate, trace them with your small-tipped, black marking pen. Let the ink dry thoroughly (3-4 minutes) before doing anything more with this page.

If you have time, follow the following directions. If not, file the page under Lesson 2. We'll come back to it later.

After the ink is dry, erase any visible pencil lines. Then color your page. Remember, white is a color, too. Leaving areas uncolored can provide a powerful visual effect. Most likely you won't have time to finish (most people took about an hour to color the whole thing). Remember to leave time to clean up.

Squares of Different Patterns • Lesson 2 • Exercise 2-A

LESSON THREE
Eagle Exercise 3-A

Instruction:

SUPPLIES NEEDED:

1. Quiet, well-lit place to work
2. Pencil
3. Sharpener
4. Eraser

What you see in the exercise section of this lesson are three pages, one with a small square window in it, one with an empty grid, and one with an eagle on the grid. Your job is to duplicate the eagle on the empty grid. Is it overwhelming? It is, if you try to tackle it all at once.

Stephanie used to say, "I'm worried about being eighty years old" (she was twenty-four at the time). She was afraid she'd wake up one day, be eighty, and not be prepared. Then it occurred to her that people don't go from twenty-four to eighty in a day or two; she would have years and years to get there, and, once she was there, she'd know how to be.

If you look at all the unknowns in your life ahead (College? Marriage? To whom? Job? Children? When? How many? House? Where? Ministry? Retirement? When?), you will be overwhelmed. That's why God doesn't show it to you all at once. Day by day, minute by minute, you do the next thing. So it is with this exercise. You do it little by little, one square at a time.

If you were drawing an eagle freehand with your Left Brain, you'd probably start with the head and then draw the beak, neck, wings, etc. The Left Brain likes to start with what's important to it. The Right Brain doesn't assign value or worth. To the Right Brain, everything is interesting; things don't have to "mean" or "be" anything. It can enjoy just looking at color or texture or line. The Right Brain also doesn't mind starting in the middle, on the bottom, on the edge. There isn't anything that's "more important"–although it may find some colors or shapes more interesting than others.

Exercise 3-A

Notice the square that is cut out of the page on Sheet 3-A. This creates a small window. With this window you will be able to look at the grid one square at a time. You may choose not to use it, but you have the option to use it if you start to feel overwhelmed.

Were you able to do the last exercise? You copied lines and spaces into the boxes. This is the same kind of thing. Each square on the grid is a box. All you have to do is copy the light and dark shapes into the boxes on the other grid.

Operating on the Left Brain is like walking. You can walk in any direction as long as it's on a surface. Operating on the Right Brain is like swimming. You can go any direction, up, down, sideways. So, to start this exercise, pick any square on the eagle and copy what's in it into the corresponding square on the blank grid. For example, if you want to start with the tip of the eagle's right wing your starting square on the empty grid would be C-2. Use light lines at first, make your evaluations and corrections, erase, and then shade in the dark areas to match the original.

Eagle • Lesson 3

Example: Enlarged to show detail.

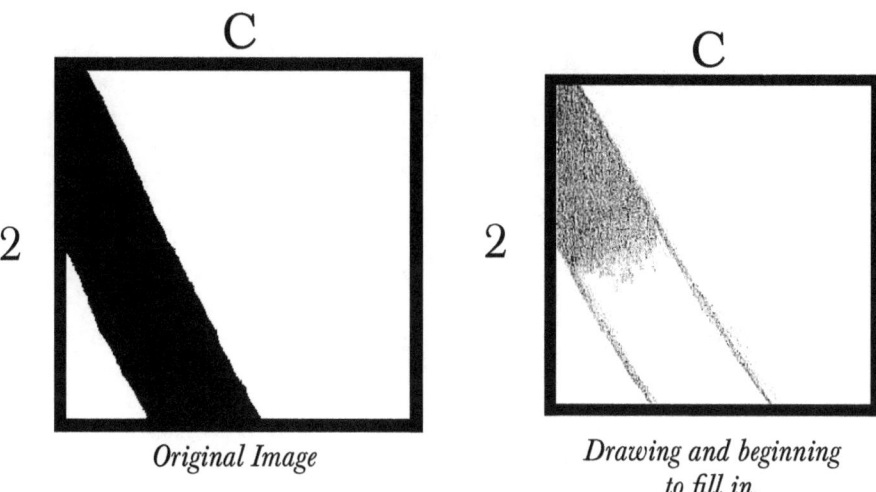

Original Image   *Drawing and beginning to fill in.*

When you're done, look at the whole thing. Is it pretty close to looking like an eagle? It may not be perfect, but it's probably better than you could have done just trying to copy the whole image. Take a moment to evaluate:

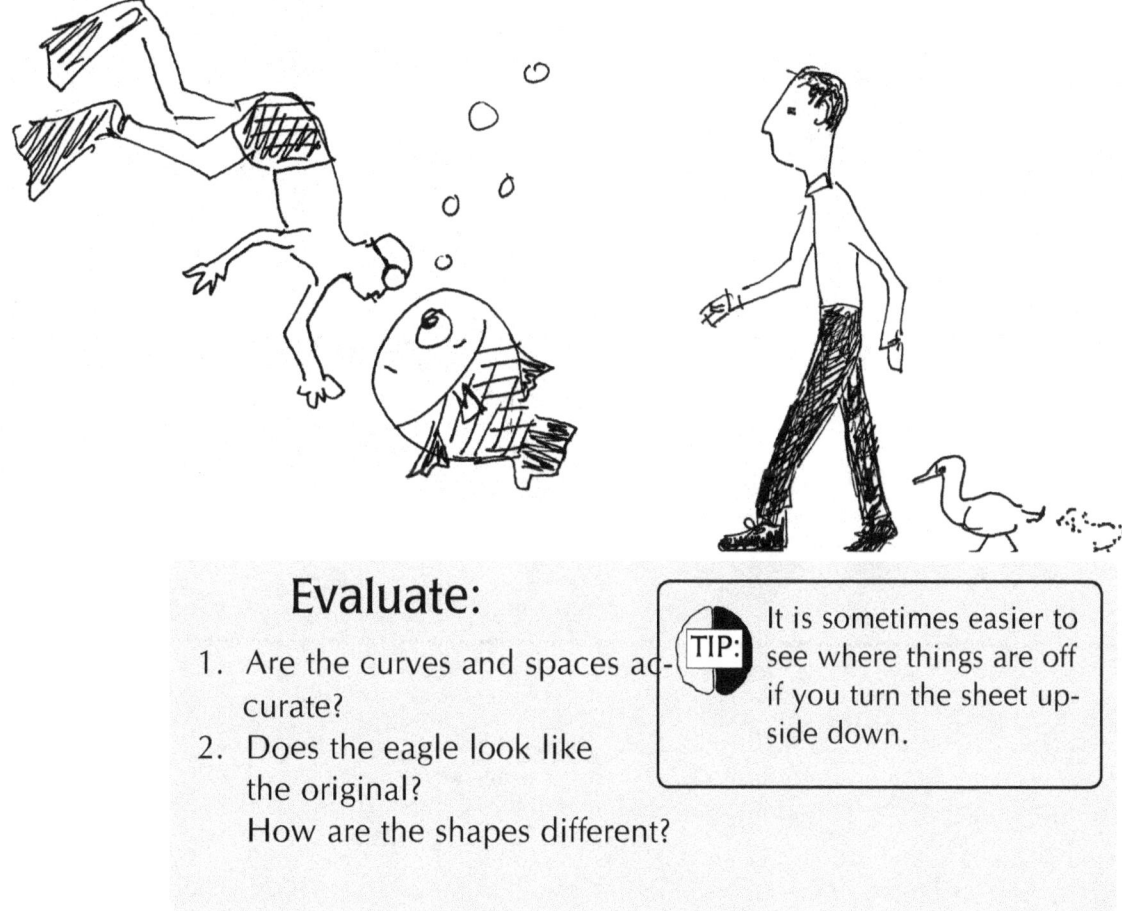

Evaluate:

1. Are the curves and spaces accurate?
2. Does the eagle look like the original?
   How are the shapes different?

TIP: It is sometimes easier to see where things are off if you turn the sheet upside down.

Eagle • Lesson 3

Eagle • Lesson 3 • Exercise 3-A
Loose-leaf sheets for each Exercise are available for printing at www.earthen.com/exercises/

	A	B	C	D	E	F	G	H	I	J	K	L	M	N
1														
2														
3														
4														
5														
6														
7														
8														
9														
10														
11														
12														
13														
14														
15														
16														
17														
18														
19														

Loose-leaf sheets for each Exercise are available for printing at www.earthen.com/exercises/

LESSON FOUR

Proportion Squares
Exercises 4-A, 4-B, 4-C

Instruction:

SUPPLIES NEEDED:

1. Quiet, well-lit place to work
2. Pencil
3. Eraser
4. Colored pencils
5. Sharpener
6. Black, small-tipped marking pen

Exercises 4-A–C

There are three sheets in this next exercise, each with a stack of boxes in three different sizes. On each sheet, duplicate the lines and spaces from the decorated box in each of the other two boxes, maintaining the relationships of lines and spaces, the proportions, the curves. Take your time. You can still measure, although you'll have to do some math.

The medium box is two times larger than the small one. The big box is four times larger than the small one. So, if you want to measure, say from the small box to the big box, take the reading on the small box and quadruple (multiply times four) the amount. Then you will be starting in the proper place proportionately.

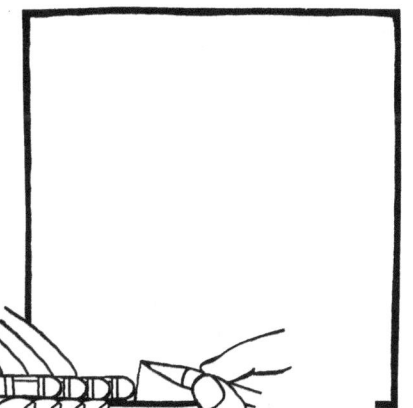

When you are done with Exercise 4-A, evaluate your work. Have you drawn the curves to look like the original, preserving the relationships between the lines, spaces, and the borders of the box? Go back and fix anything which seems off to you. Then ink the pencil lines. Get up and stretch, take some deep breaths, get your blood moving. By then your ink should have dried (if you do thick, juicy lines, it takes longer). Now erase the pencil marks.

It's really important that you let the ink dry completely before erasing. Many a beautiful drawing has been smeared by hasty erasing.

Follow this same procedure for Sheets A-B and C When you are finished with the inking process, go ahead and color to your heart's content. If you run out of time, save the sheets for the next lesson.

Be sure to leave enough time to clean up.

 Sometimes artists troubleshoot their pictures by looking at them in a mirror. Remember you can also evaluate by turning your picture upside-down.

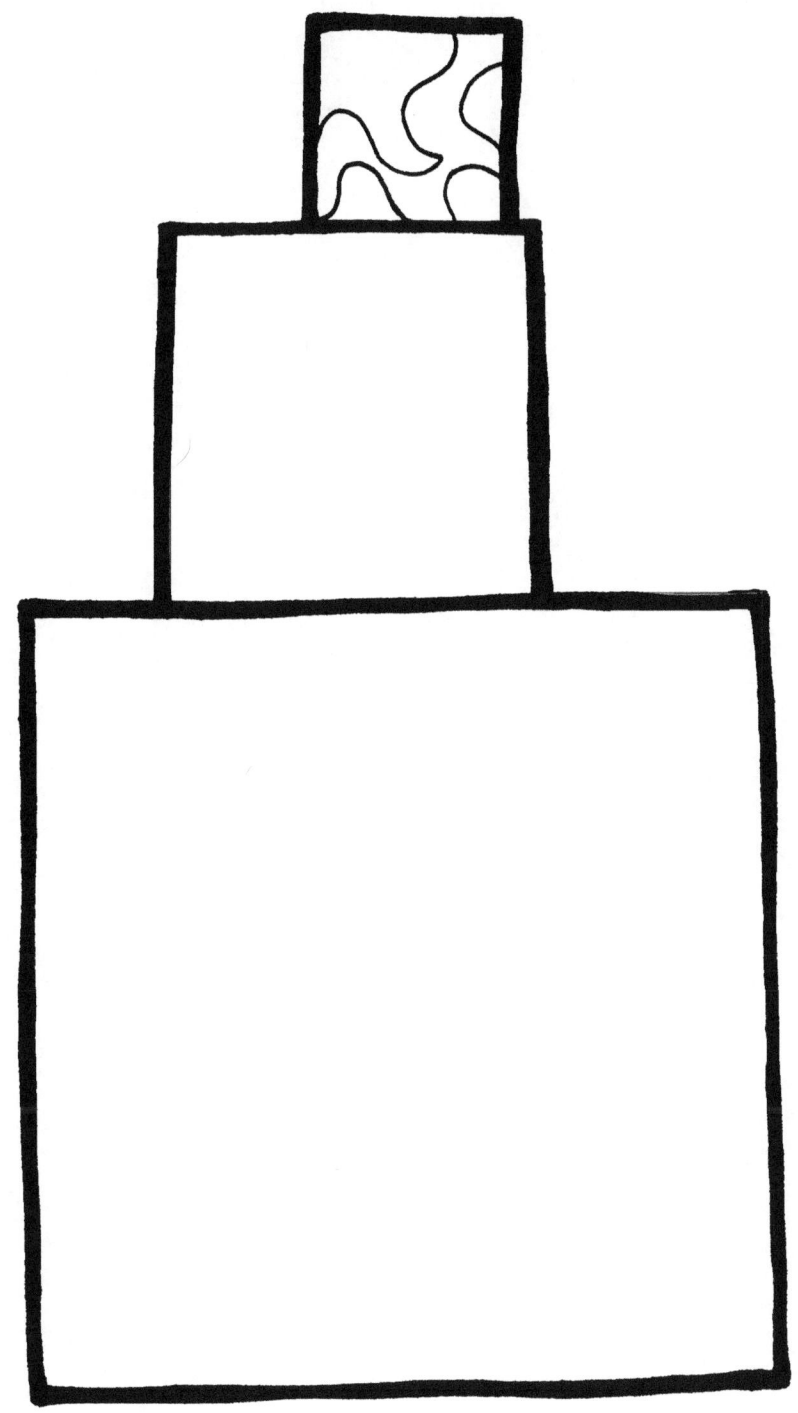

Proportion Squares • Lesson 4 • Exercise 4-A

Proportion Squares • Lesson 4 • Exercise 4-B

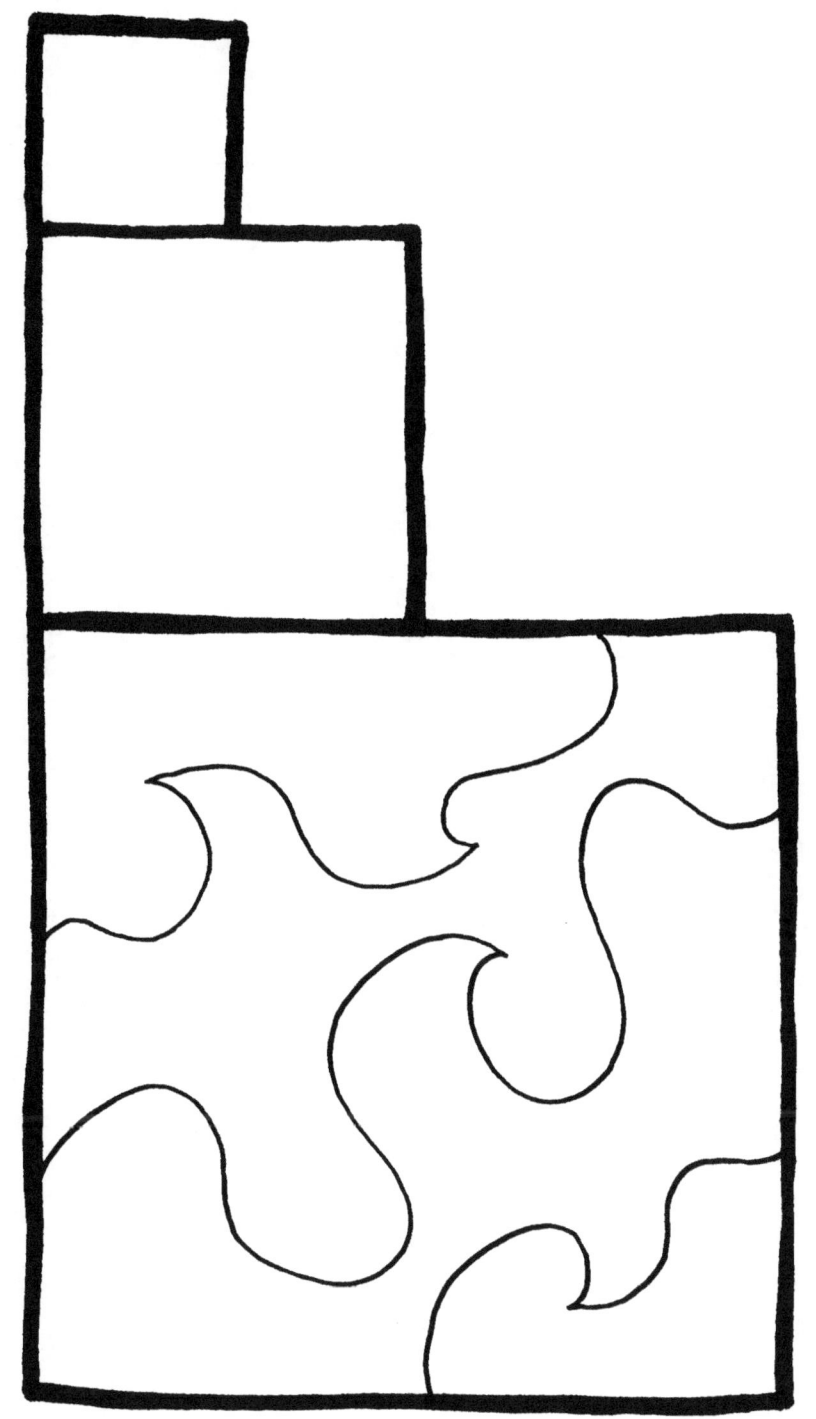

LESSON FIVE *Time to Color*

Instruction:

SUPPLIES NEEDED:

1. Quiet, well-lit place to work
2. Sharpener
3. Colored pencils or fine-tipped colored marking pens

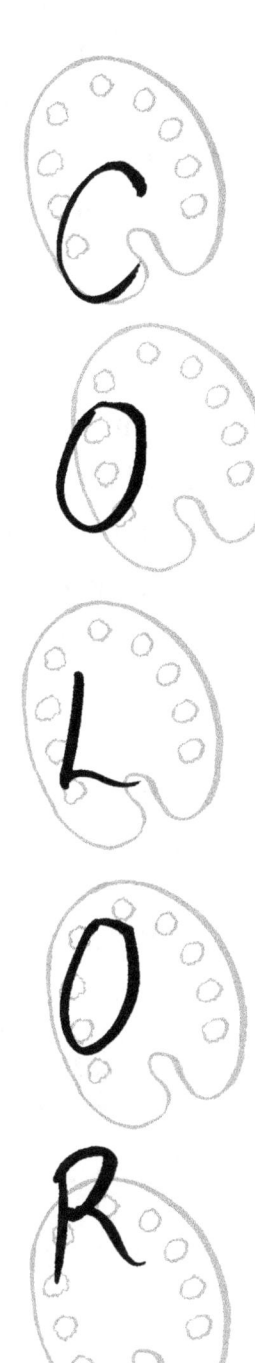

Have you finished coloring all your pages, or are you beginning to feel buried under a pile of half-completed papers? Here is your chance to catch up. If you've finished everything, you may go to Lesson 6, but not until you've read the text of this lesson.

One of the things we noticed as we developed this course is that the older people had trouble with this lesson. They felt guilty. This is not surprising when you consider that a number of the Art Course Guinea Pigs were adults. Even for Stephanie and me, who love art, it didn't seem right that we could take an hour out of a busy business day to sit and color. It wasn't "work"—we were having too much fun. On the other hand, Lynne said she felt she should have been folding laundry or cleaning the kitchen. Anything else would have been more useful. Now, the fact that the laundry was being folded by another family member and the kitchen was already clean made no difference. She had the belief that artistic pursuits were a waste of time. She did not get enjoyment out of putting color in the squares; her only satisfaction at the completion of the task was that it was over.

You may not have any problems with coloring—either feeling guilty because you're having fun instead of "working," or feeling hostile because it is a waste of time. Remember this is an art course. Coloring is part of the assignment. You HAVE to do it, and you have to do it ALL. You can't cut corners (fulfilling the letter of the Law, but not the spirit) by coloring the entire sheet blue (as one of our younger Guinea Pigs threatened to do). You must work with combinations of colors. This is work. We are not saying you have to enjoy it. It takes time and cramps up your hand. But it helps stimulate your Right Brain and gives you new neural pathways so you can think more fully and solve your problems in any area from new and unexpected angles.

It is also a known fact that colors, with their different wave lengths, have different effects on the brain. Blue is restful and calming. Yellow is good for the nervous system. When you spend time concentrating on color, you are stimulating your Right Brain, resting your Left Brain, and opening your imagination. It also helps you relax. It's impossible to color and worry.

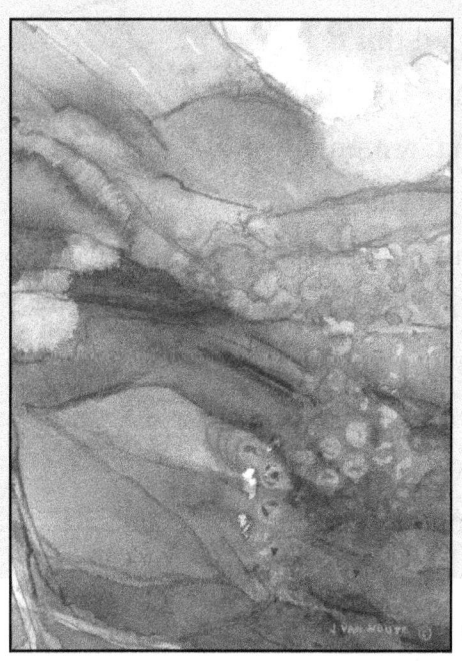

Joyce Van Houte. *Mini Abstract #11*. 1996. Watercolor , 6" x 8". Private Collection.

Abstract painting celebrates colors, shapes, nuances, textures, and relationships rather than identifiable things. To people used to operating only on their label-making Left Brains, abstracts are boring, meaningless, and stupid. If you hear people saying these things, there's a good chance they have not developed their Right Brains very much.

Use this lesson time to finish coloring the sheets from Lessons 1, 2 and 4.

LESSON SIX
Silhouetted Tree
Exercise 6-A

Instruction:

SUPPLIES NEEDED:

1. Quiet, well-lit place to work
2. Pencil
3. Eraser
4. Colored pencils
5. Sharpener
6. Black, small-tipped marking pen

In the old days, there were no copy machines. If you wanted to make a drawing larger, you couldn't just flop it on the glass, push a button, and get an image 65% bigger. How did they do it? They used grids.

Exercise 6-A

You already know how to copy from one box into another box of the same size. You also know how to enlarge. In this exercise, copy the tree onto the enlargement grid, one square at a time.

The Left Brain, so anxious to identify, categorize, and label, is also the side that stresses out if it can't get the drawing to look like the item identified. Its preoccupation with the facts and the actuality of the thing keeps it from being able to see what the thing really looks like. So take your time. Don't be distracted or worry about whether it looks like a tree. Just keep copying, as accurately as you can, the lines and spaces from one box into the other. If looking at the whole image confuses you, feel free to use the sheet with the small window. Also remember you can measure and rotate your paper. Use short, light, feathery strokes.

Silhouetted Tree • Lesson 6

When you're done, evaluate. Correct. Ink the lines, let them dry, and color to your heart's content.

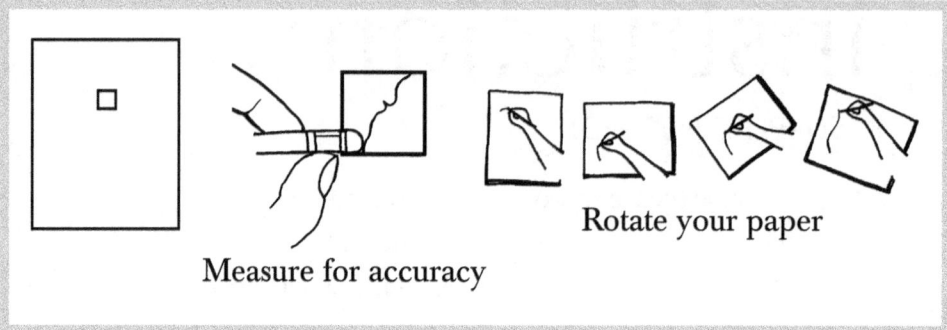

Measure for accuracy

Rotate your paper

Silhouetted Tree • Lesson 6

Silhouetted Tree • Lesson 6 • Exercise 6-A

47

	A	B	C	D	E	F	G	H
1								
2								
3								
4								
5								
6								
7								
8								
9								

Silhouetted Tree • Lesson 6 • Exercise 6-A

Loose-leaf sheets for each Exercise are available for printing at www.earthen.com/exercises/

LESSON SEVEN
Contour Drawing • 7-A, 7-B, 7-C, 7-D, 7-E, 7-F

I haven't skated for at least forty years. If I laced up a pair of skates and stepped out on the ice, how do you think I'd do? When I was a teenager, I took lessons for a couple of years and knew how to spin and jump, but now I would probably just break bones.

When you start to learn a skill, it flashes an impulse across the neurons– a weak signal at first. If you continue to learn the skill, the impulses get stronger and stronger. New nerves grow to accomodate the new signals. Eventually, the pathway becomes a superhighway. But if you don't use a skill, no signals flash across the neuron and the pathway eventually disconnects and falls away.

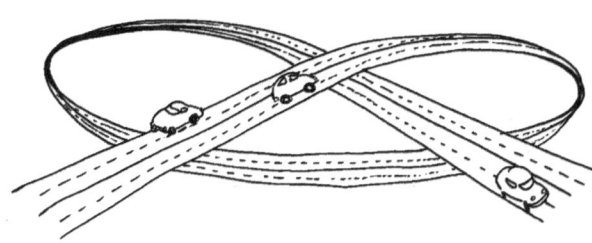

These exercises will help build neural pathways for seeing detail.

Some kinds of work require accuracy in observation. A surgeon must make sure he removes all the diseased tissue, has stitched everything back up properly, and hasn't left any sponges or instruments in the patient. An auto mechanic must monitor the instruments carefully, checking for any abnormal changes. Mothers are like detectives. They have to see everything and remember what they saw. If the baby is playing with five small buttons and the next time you look there are only three, what do you think might have happened?

Of course you wouldn't let the baby play with small buttons anyway. It was only an example.

Some people love to do detailed work. They can sit for hours adding columns of figures without making mistakes. Others enjoy drawing hair on the cat or carefully constructing a model—sanding, painting, positioning decals. To others, detailed work is boring, tedious (seems like it goes on forever and is a lot more trouble than it's worth), and tiresome. They want to finish the job and get on with the program. You have both kinds of thinking in your head.

Q: When you hear yourself thinking, "This is too hard!" or "I'm tired of doing this," which half of your brain is talking?

A: _____

If you have a highly developed Left Brain and underdeveloped Right Brain, this next exercise will drive you nuts. It won't make sense. You will want to keep peeking to make sure you're on track. But just trust and obey. Your Right Brain loves details and needs to be stimulated with "looking" in order to develop neuralpathways. The more you learn to look, the more you'll begin to see. The more you see, the easier it will be to see more. You may even find yourself feeling the delight of timelessness. That's a sure sign you're operating in the Right Brain. The Left Brain is the clock-watcher. The Right Brain could care less. (But that's not an excuse to be late.)

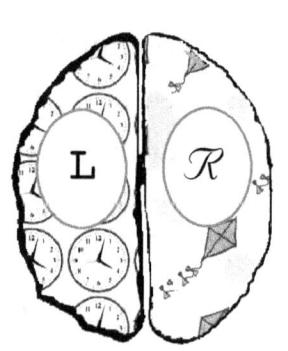

Instruction:

SUPPLIES NEEDED:

1. Quiet, well-lit place to work
2. Pencil
3. Paper
4. Tape
5. Flower
6. Paper Bag

WHAT IS A CONTOUR DRAWING?

A contour drawing is a record of detail—each fold, wrinkle, edge, and change. Picture a mountain scene with white clouds in blue sky, tall green trees with a little house under their branches. The place where the mountains meet the sky, where the sky meets the clouds, where the trees meet the mountain and the house meets the trees—these are all edges. They can also be called "contours."

Now look at your hand. See all the wrinkles in it? Look at the creases where your fingers bend. Notice the lines in your palm. Look at the places where your fingers overlap, one over the other, and the space between the thumb and your other fingers. These are all contours. Make your hand into a fist and observe the way your skin folds where the little finger meets your palm.

Before you do the next exercise, first read all the directions. If you have any questions, ask them before you start. Do not ask any when you are drawing. Don't even mutter to yourself because that keeps the Left Brain in action.

Contour Drawing • Lesson 7

Exercise **7-A**

Flower

HOW TO DO A CONTOUR DRAWING:

1. Tape a sheet of white paper to your desk on the area that you usually do your writing. Put a piece of tape on each edge of the paper to keep it from moving around when you draw.

2. Turn your chair around so you're facing away from your desk, but not so far that you're uncomfortable. You're going to have to sit this way for quite some time.

3. Place your drawing hand (the one with the pencil) somewhere near the center of the paper.

4. In your other hand, hold the flower in a comfortable position. You may either hold it up so you can see it well, or let it rest in your lap. Do not turn the flower while you draw; hold it still and steady.

5. Keeping your body turned away from your drawing, keeping your eyes glued to the flower, begin drawing. Draw very slowly, recording each tiny bump, curve, or crease. Be as careful to be accurate in detail as you were when you copied the eagle. Pay close attention to the direction of the shapes on the flower–feeling them with your eyes as you draw them.

6. Do not lift your pencil off the paper and do not check back if you go off the edge. If you go off the edge, place your pencil back on the paper without looking and resume drawing.

When you're done, you may look at your drawing. It might look something like this:

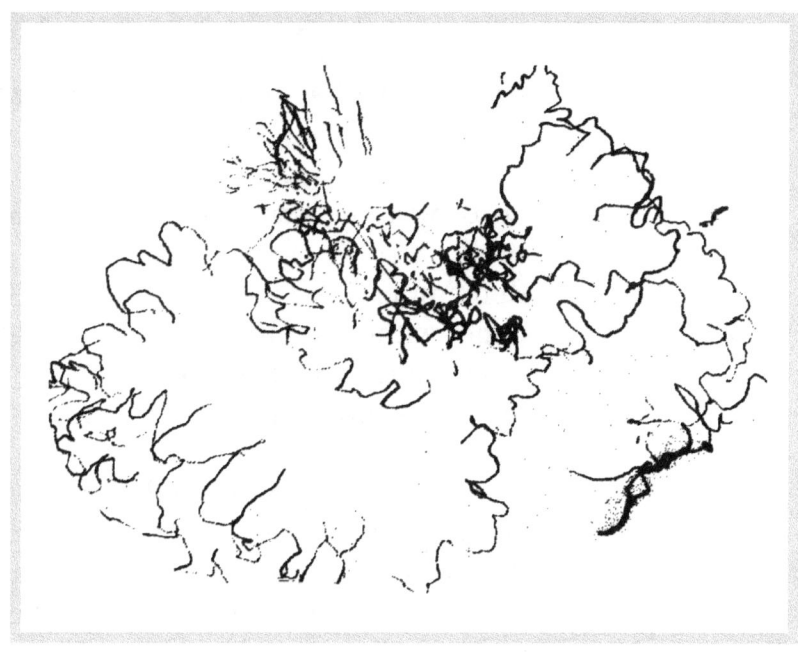

Stephanie Boyette
Age: 11

Or this:

Carolyn Wing Greenlee
Age: 35

Contour Drawing • Lesson 7

Exercise 7-B

Paper Bag

1. Wad a paper bag or a piece of paper up. Then hold it steady or place it in your lap.

2. Looking at the wrinkled object, follow the same directions as before.

3. Remember, if your pencil strays off the paper, just put it back on the paper without looking. It doesn't matter if it's in the right place. The object of the exercise is to SEE accurately and thoroughly, not to end up with a proportionate drawing.

4. Be sure to take your time. If you go slowly and do your very best, you will improve more quickly in your drawing than if you rush through the exercise. Learn each skill thoroughly so you will have a firm foundation for the next task (they build one upon the other). The object is not to do them quickly, but to do them thoroughly and well.

Carolyn Wing Greenlee

Paper Bag

Exercise 7-C

Hand

Last chance. Follow the same procedures as before, using as your model your hand (the one without the pencil). If your drawing looks too much like the actual object, it shows that you didn't do it right.

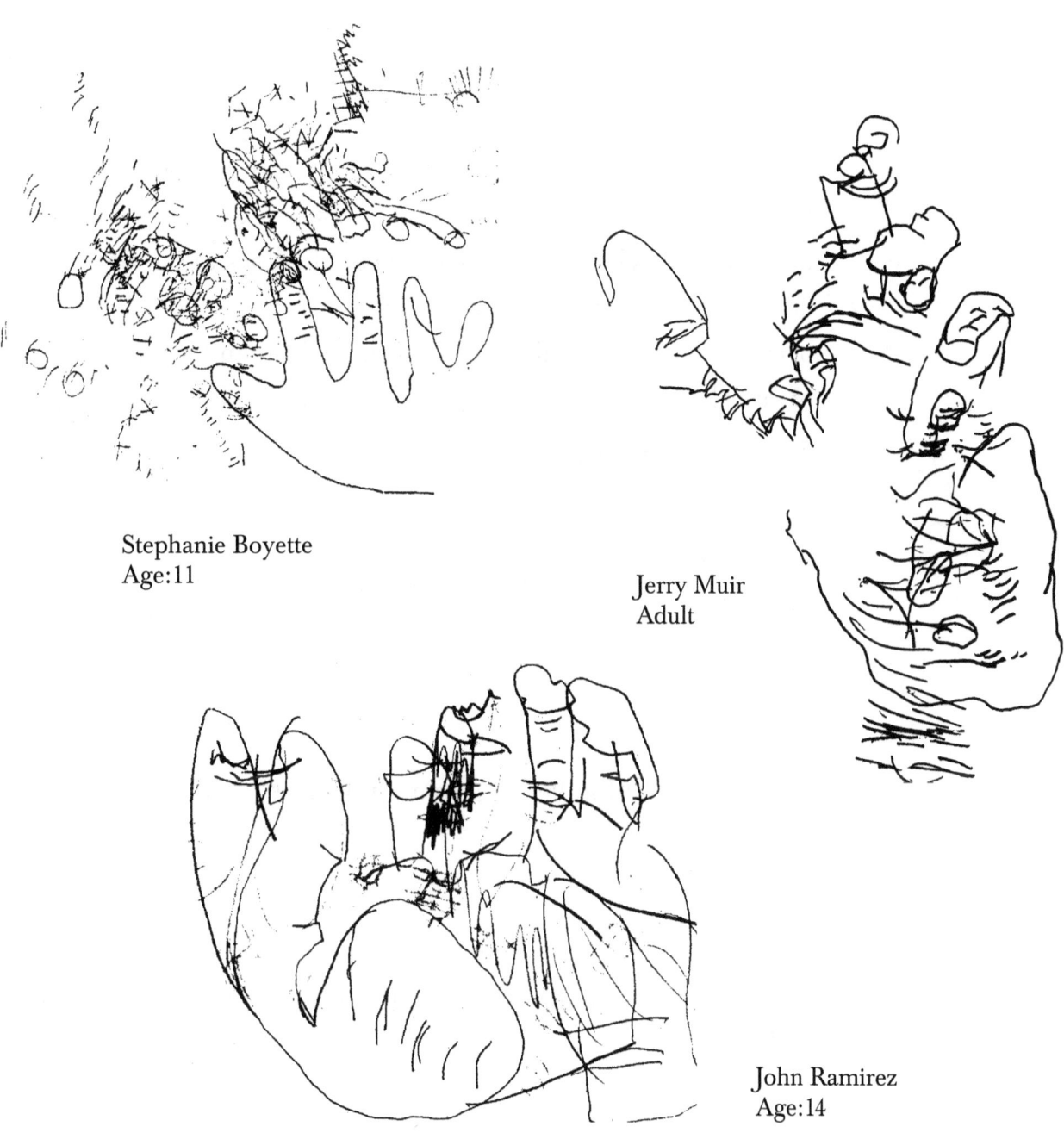

Stephanie Boyette
Age:11

Jerry Muir
Adult

John Ramirez
Age:14

Contour Drawing • Lesson 7

Instruction:

SUPPLIES NEEDED:

1. Quiet, well-lit place to work
2. Pencil
3. Paper
4. Tape
5. Tape Dispenser or Scissors
6. Flower

MODIFIED CONTOUR DRAWINGS

Modified contour drawings are done with the same careful observation and attention to detail as contour drawings, but you may glance back at your paper to keep the lines in the right relationships. These pictures will look much better to your Left Brain because the objects will be recognizable. Remember to do most of your looking at the object, however, and not at your paper. You may sit facing your drawing.

Exercise 7-D — Modified Contour Drawing #1: Draw your tape dispenser or a pair of scissors

Exercise 7-E — Modified Contour Drawing #2: Draw a flower

Exercise 7-F — Modified Contour Drawing #3: Draw your hand

Examples of modified contour drawings.

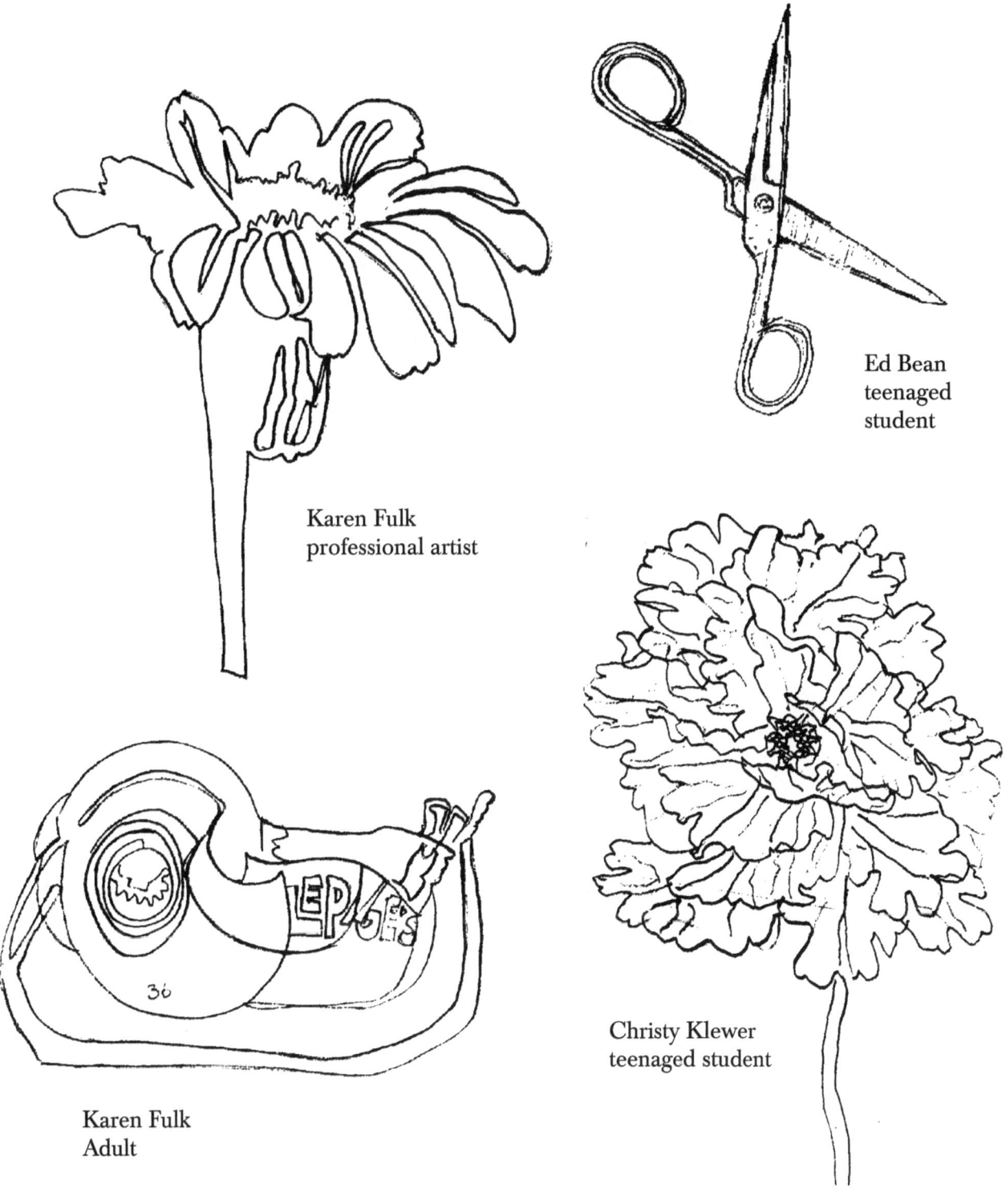

Karen Fulk
professional artist

Ed Bean
teenaged student

Karen Fulk
Adult

Christy Klewer
teenaged student

LESSON EIGHT
Covered Object • Exercise 8-A

You have just been selected by the Museum of Natural History to assist the curator of marine biology in a difficult project. Your job is to do detailed, accurate drawings of the radiolaria (a type of marine protozoa) on the slides. You look into the eyepiece of the curator's micro-scope. What you see looks like this:

How will you ever do it?

With a sinking feeling, you take your position at the table and stare through the microscope at the intricate structures on your slide. Your radiolaria are stunningly beautiful, like little crystal helmets and space ships, but you wonder how you will copy them. Then, suddenly you realize that you really do have the skills you need.

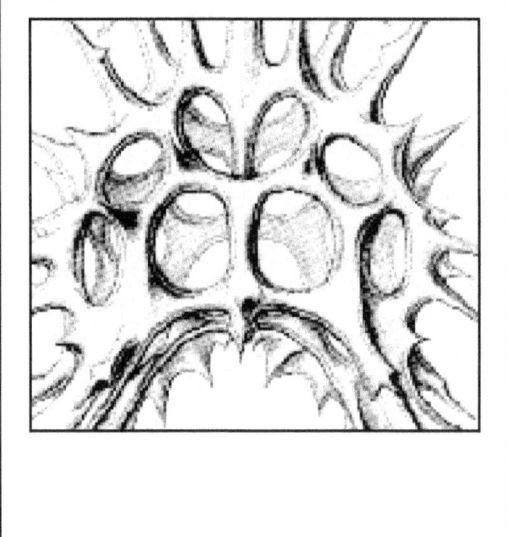

You have already learned how to see objects in terms of the relationships of lines and spaces. You know that all you have to do is turn on your Right Brain and turn down the Left. But how? The array of complex forms is intimidating. Where should you begin?

Then you have an idea. With a special Polaroid camera, you take quick pictures of the radiolaria, which you send to the museum photographic lab for enlargement. Conveniently, it's just down the hall.

Covered Object • Lesson 8   **61**

Instruction:

SUPPLIES NEEDED:

1. Quiet, well-lit place to work
2. Pencil
3. Sharpener
4. Two sheets of paper

Exercise 8-A

The lab sends you an image marked 8-A. You look at the print and decide which of the four you will draw first.

Having made your selection, you cover it with a piece of paper. Starting from the top, you slide the paper down just enough so you can see a little bit of the form. You sharpen your pencil and take a deep breath. Carefully, on a separate sheet of paper, you begin to draw what you see. Then you repeat the process, exposing only a little of the form at a time. This way, your Right Brain sees the relationships, but your Left Brain can't make enough sense of the object to become confused or overwhelmed. Using feathery strokes, you continue this way until you have completed the form.

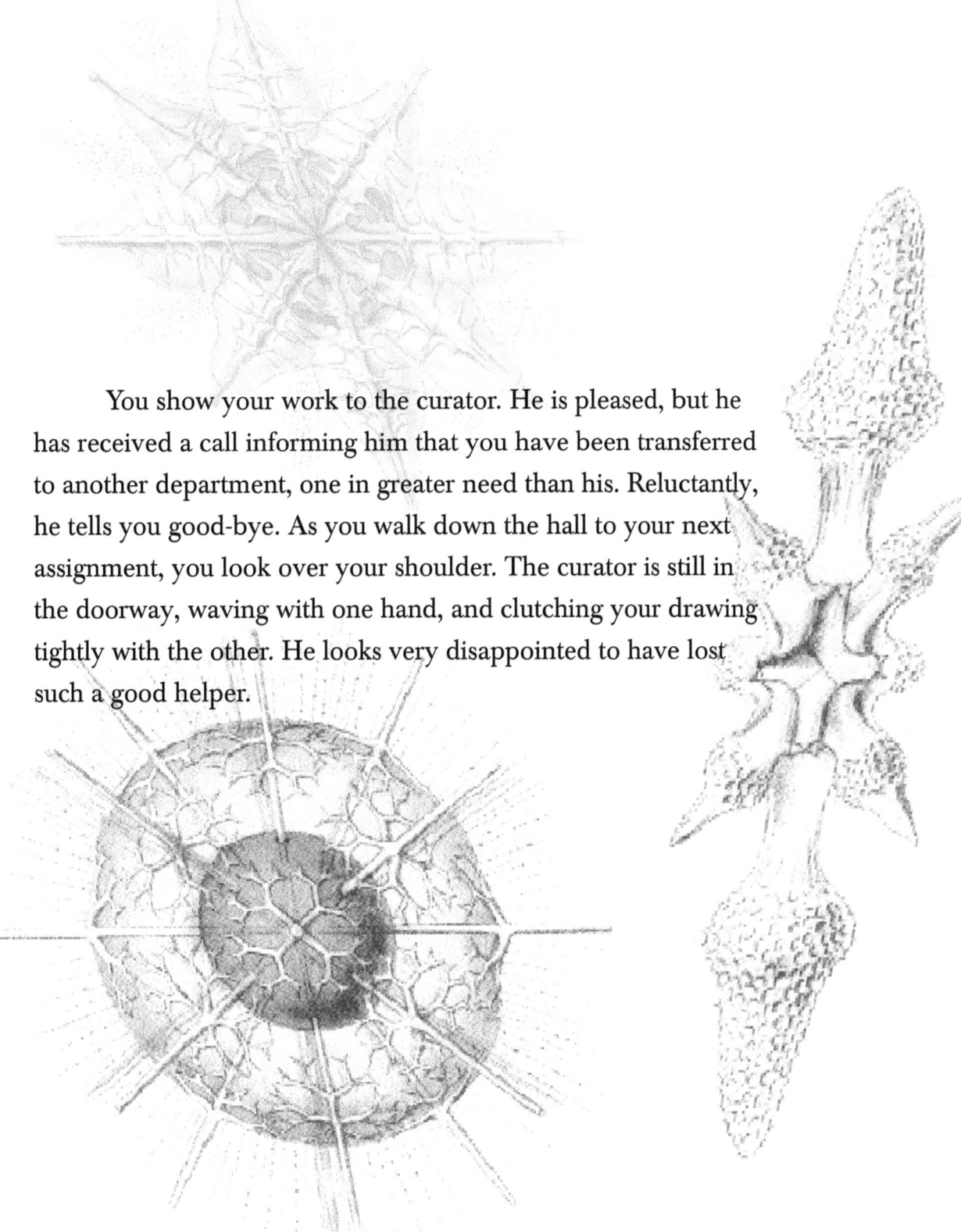

You show your work to the curator. He is pleased, but he has received a call informing him that you have been transferred to another department, one in greater need than his. Reluctantly, he tells you good-bye. As you walk down the hall to your next assignment, you look over your shoulder. The curator is still in the doorway, waving with one hand, and clutching your drawing tightly with the other. He looks very disappointed to have lost such a good helper.

Images are various species of radiolaria (a type of marine protozoa).

Covered Object • Lesson 8

8-A

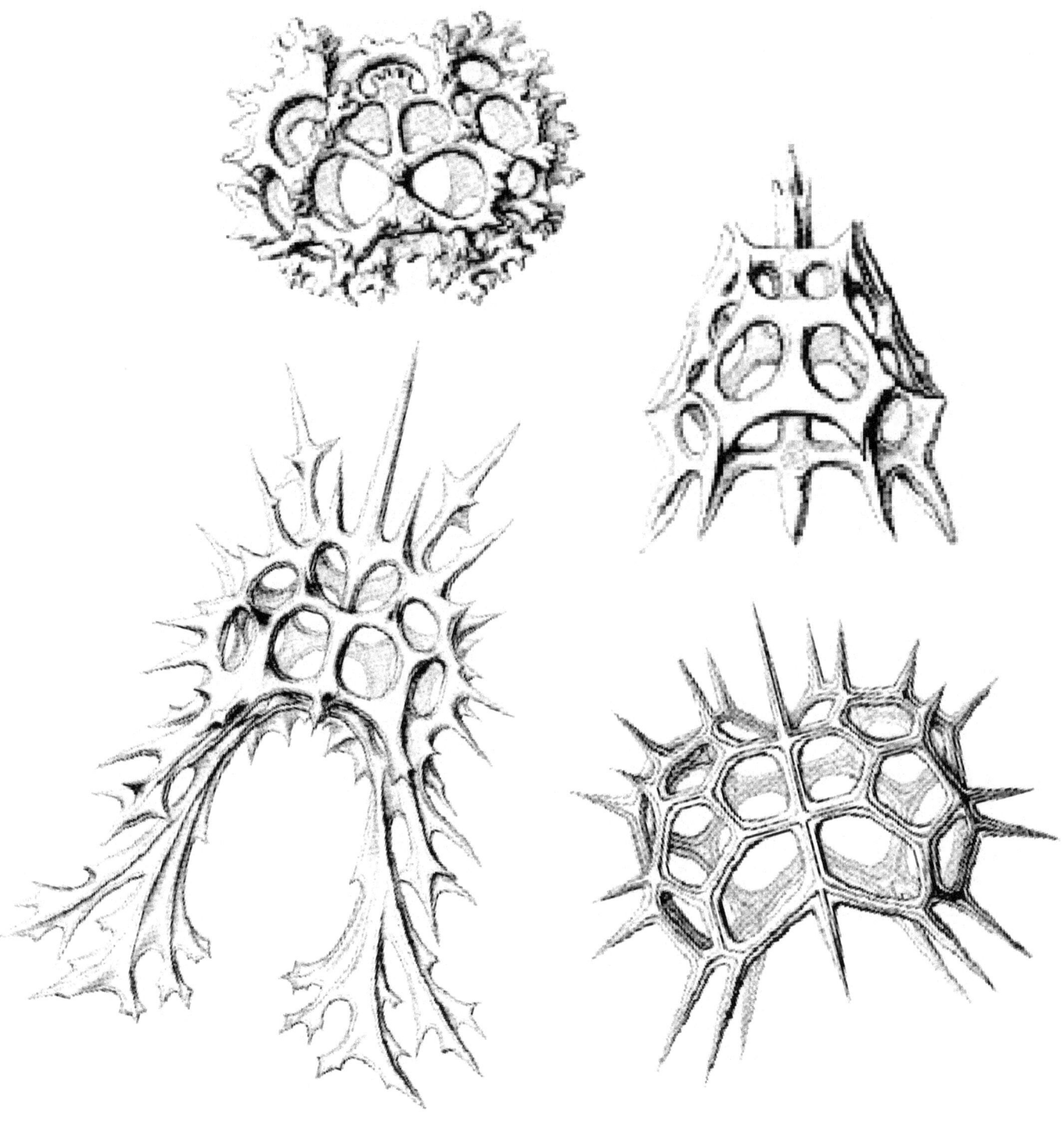

LESSON NINE

*Upside-Down
Exercise 9-A*

Your new assignment is with the curator of nocturnal mammals. She hands you some photographs.

In shock, you see this:

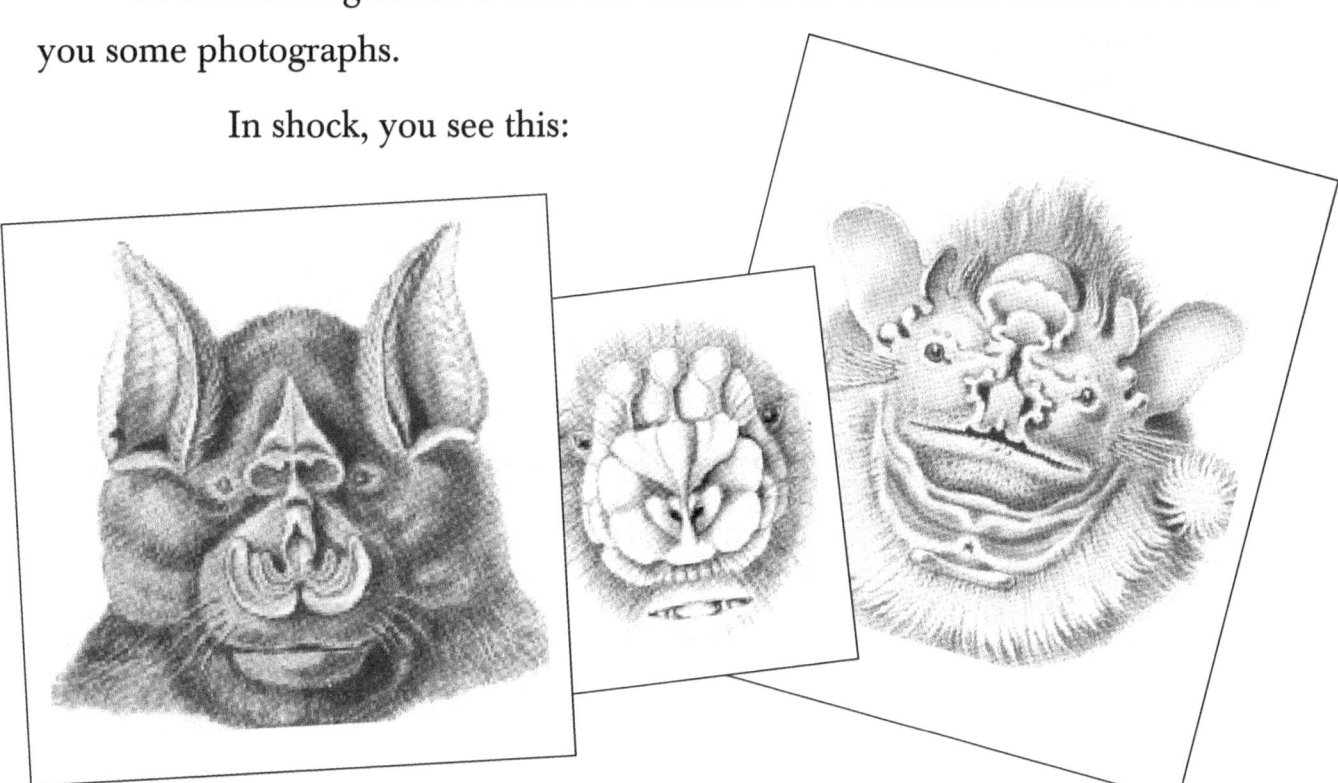

You check the door. Is this the right place? Have you stumbled into a lab where they study nocturnal mammals, or alien creatures? You guess they are the faces of

_____. You name them _____,

_____ and _____.

Actually, they are faces of bats. Once again, your assignment is to draw these complex creatures. You make your selection and begin to draw but your Left Brain sees the face and keeps confusing you. You try covering it, but it still looks too much like a face. Then you have another great idea. Knowing that the Left Brain wants to label whatever it recognizes, you figure out a way to make the face unrecognizable: you turn the photograph upside-down. That's much better. You are just about to begin, but wait a minute. . .

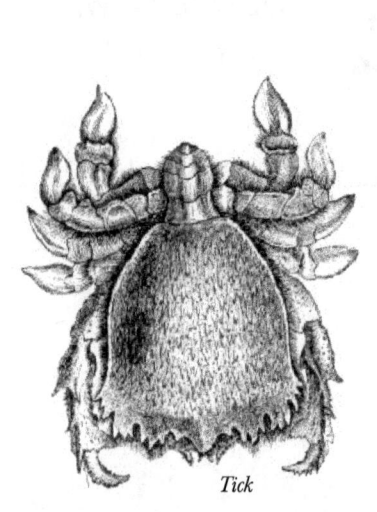
Tick

Siphonophors - hydras class

The curator is telling you that there's been another transfer. They need you across the hall in Amphibians. Crystal space ships, alien monsters…what amazing beasts could await you in Room 686?

Dinoflagellata (formerly considered to be unicellular plants)

Worm

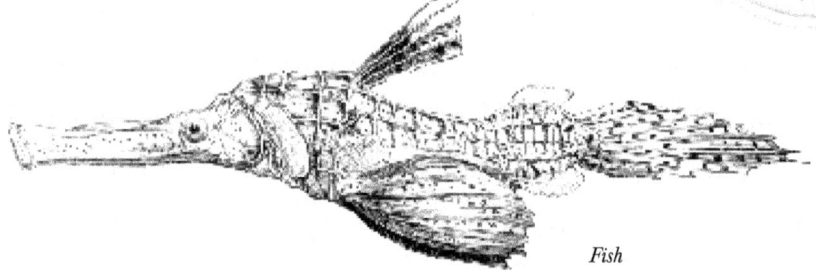
Fish

68 Upside-Down • Lesson 9

Instruction:

SUPPLIES NEEDED:

1. Quiet, well-lit place to work
2. Pencil
3. Sharpener
4. Paper

When you check in at Room 686, you are breathless with anticipation. The curator hands you the pictures that you must copy. You look at them in dismay. Frogs!

How boring! Common frogs. Not even exotic poisonous red and blue tree frogs. You are disappointed. You have drawn complex radiolaria. You had even figured out how to draw the dreaded bat face. Now you are doing frogs. It is like being demoted.

You choose one of the frogs and start to draw. You think: eyeball, snout, back… Your mind wanders to the next football game, the traffic noises outside. You finish very quickly. You're proud of that. Then you notice that the drawing is warped, distorted. It looks like a cartoon. You realize your Left Brain, happy to be drawing something recognizeable and easy, has overridden

your Right. It drew the most important things first and then the parts that all frogs have, paying little attention to the actual proportions or details of this particular frog. In scientific illustration this will never do. You sigh. This is harder than you thought. How will you solve the problem? How did you do it before? What would you do if this were a more difficult subject? Then you remember the procedure you worked out for the bat faces. You try turning the frog picture upside down and uncovering a little bit at a time. You observe every curve, every relationship of line and space. You take your time, careful to look at what is really there.

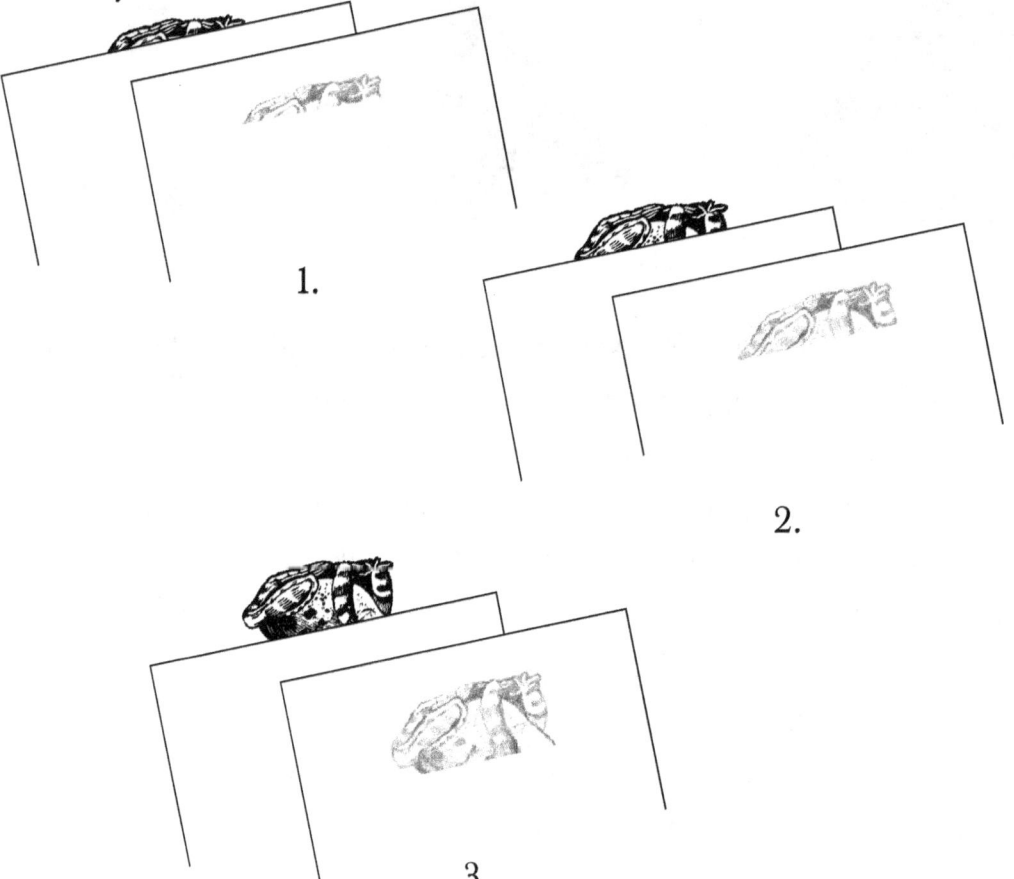

1.

2.

3.

Upside-Down • Lesson 9

Exercise 9-A

Select a frog. Turn it upside down. Cover it with a sheet of paper. Draw a little at a time, uncovering portions of the object as you finish the part you can see. Don't try to label or identify what you are drawing. Remember to just look at relationships, curves and lines.

The curator inspects your drawing and rewards you with a big smile. "We are having a great number of startling discoveries in the amphibian world," he explains. We cannot waste our time with people who cannot render accurate drawings of the new creatures. Therefore, we give our prospective helpers this simple test. We feel that those who are careful in the simple things will be careful in the complex things. You have done well. Welcome to the team!"

72

9-A

Upside Down • Lesson 9 • Exercise 9-A

9-A

LESSON TEN
Negative Space
Exercise 10-A

What do you see in this box to the left? _____
What else do you see? _____ Anything else? _____.

If you're like most people, the first thing you saw was a horse. The next thing (and this took some thinking) was the box. But what do you call the rest of the picture? Background? Air? White paper? Actually, it really does have a name. It's called "negative space."

Negative space is whatever isn't the object (or the subject). The black lines here are the negative space. If you look at the white areas instead of the black ones, you will see the subject. What does it say?

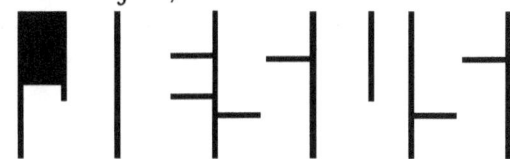

_____

In art, the area around the subject has as much form and importance as the subject itself. Especially in drawing, looking at negative space can help you see accurately. Your Right Brain enjoys negative space. Remember, shapes don't have to *be* anything to be interesting to the Right Brain; it's the shapes themselves that capture its attention. That's why it is able to see what is really there.

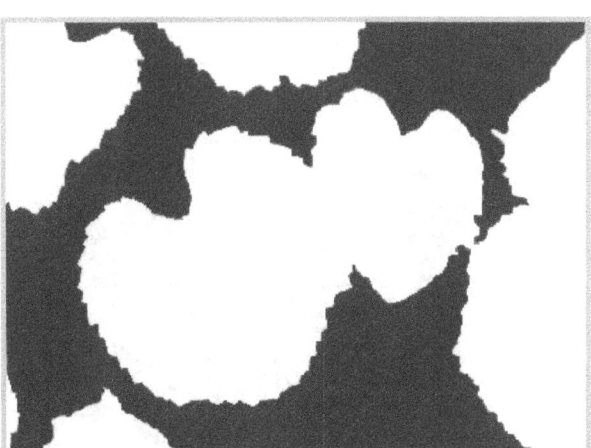

Photo © Carolyn Wing Greenlee

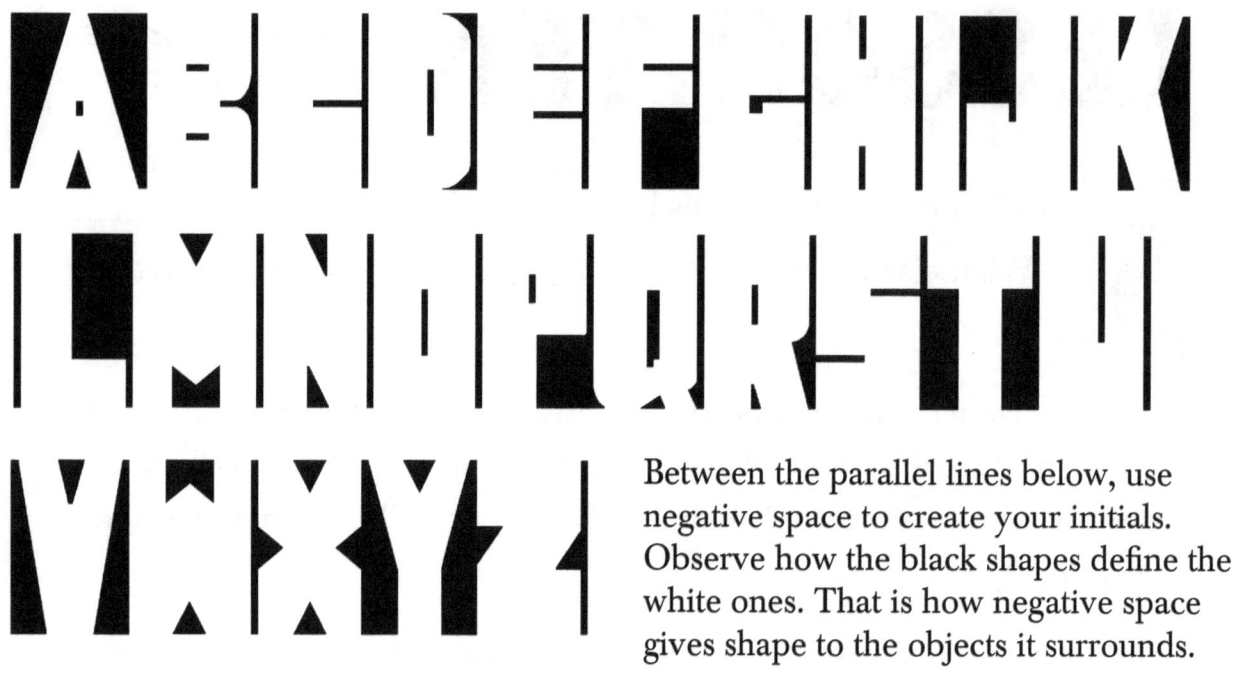

Between the parallel lines below, use negative space to create your initials. Observe how the black shapes define the white ones. That is how negative space gives shape to the objects it surrounds.

―――――――――――――――――

―――――――――――――――――

Seeing accurately is important if you are a jet pilot and have to read a lot of gauges quickly. Or if you're a policeman or a detective. Accuracy is especially important if you're doing scientific drawings. Look at these two butterflies. They seem the same, but they are actually different varities. One is a normal butterfly and one is a normal butterfly with a very bad taste. If you were a bird who eats butterflies or a scientist who studies them, it would be very important that you could tell the differences. Draw arrows from one butterfuly to the other, showing the areas of difference. There are at least ten.

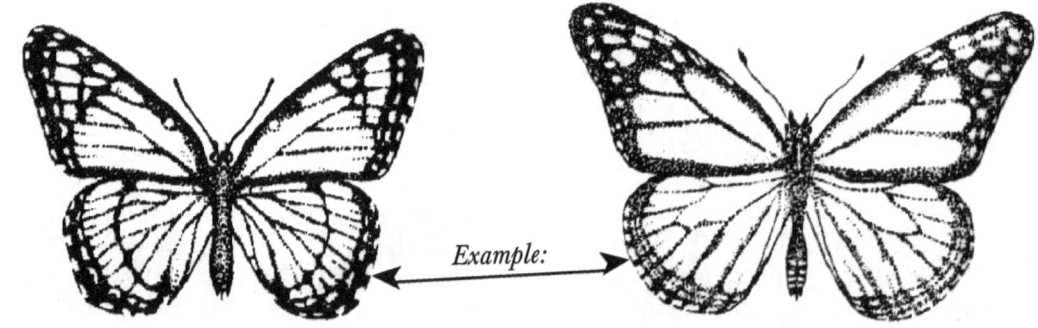

Example:

Once you see accurately, you will be able to draw accurately. Then your drawings won't be misshappen or distorted unless you choose to make them that way. Does this mean that the only good art is realistic? No. Artists throughout the ages have used exaggeration and other techniques which have heightened the emotional impact of their images, but first they learned how to draw accurately.

These are two pictures by the artist Milford Zornes. In 1944 he did this linotype of trees in Burma (left). Forty years later he did the painting of bare trees (below) with India ink. Notice how the shapes are abstracted into pure design, but they still have the feeling of the structure and vitality of a specific kind of tree..

Pictures by Milford Zornes, N.A.

Mr. Zornes says it's important to really look at your subject matter. "You look until you see the truth of it. Then you draw the line that says 'palm tree' to the viewer." Only those who have learned how to see can reveal the true nature of the subject matter.

Negative Space • Lesson 10

Instruction:

SUPPLIES NEEDED:

1. Quiet, well-lit place to work
2. Pencil with eraser
3. Paper
4. Black, small-tipped marker
5. Colored Pencils
6. Sharpener

Exercise 10-A

On sheet 10-A, you will see four boxes. Draw the white areas of the image in the empty box next to it and shade them evenly so that you have a negative of the image. Remember you may turn your paper.

Example: ⬛⬜

Exercise 10-B

You are planning to make a stained glass window of either ribbons or grass (10-B) First, on a piece of paper, you sketch the shapes that you must cut out. Remember you can measure length, width, height, and distance with your pencil (remember to use the eraser end). Use light, feathery strokes and concentrate on keeping the shapes proportionate.

Example of original image.

Example of beginning to draw the negative space shapes.

Negative Space • Lesson 10

In the empty box next to the original, you draw the shapes of the glass again, but this time each piece in relation to the other. Darken the areas between the pieces of glass with your black felt tip pen. You will end up with a replica of the original. If you have time, color the image with your colored pencils.

Original image.

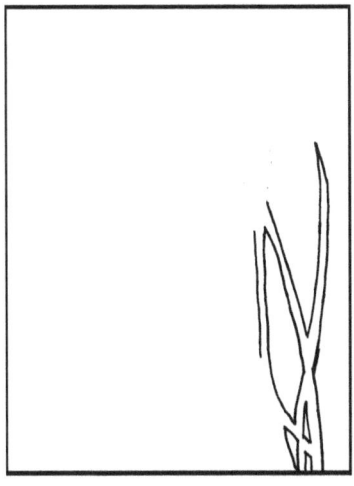
Beginning to draw the image.

Lines filled in with black and "glass" areas colored.

Exercise 10-C

From the three photographs (10-C), choose one. Carefully draw the negative space (anything that is not the mug and the bowl, the table, or the area in the window that is not the kittens or ladder).

> Negative space is one of the most important aspects of art. These exercises will help you with composition. They will help you solve difficult problems—not only in your drawings, but in the rest of your life too. Remember the neural pathways? Stimulating the Right Brain by looking at negative space will give you new ways to think. It will surprise you.

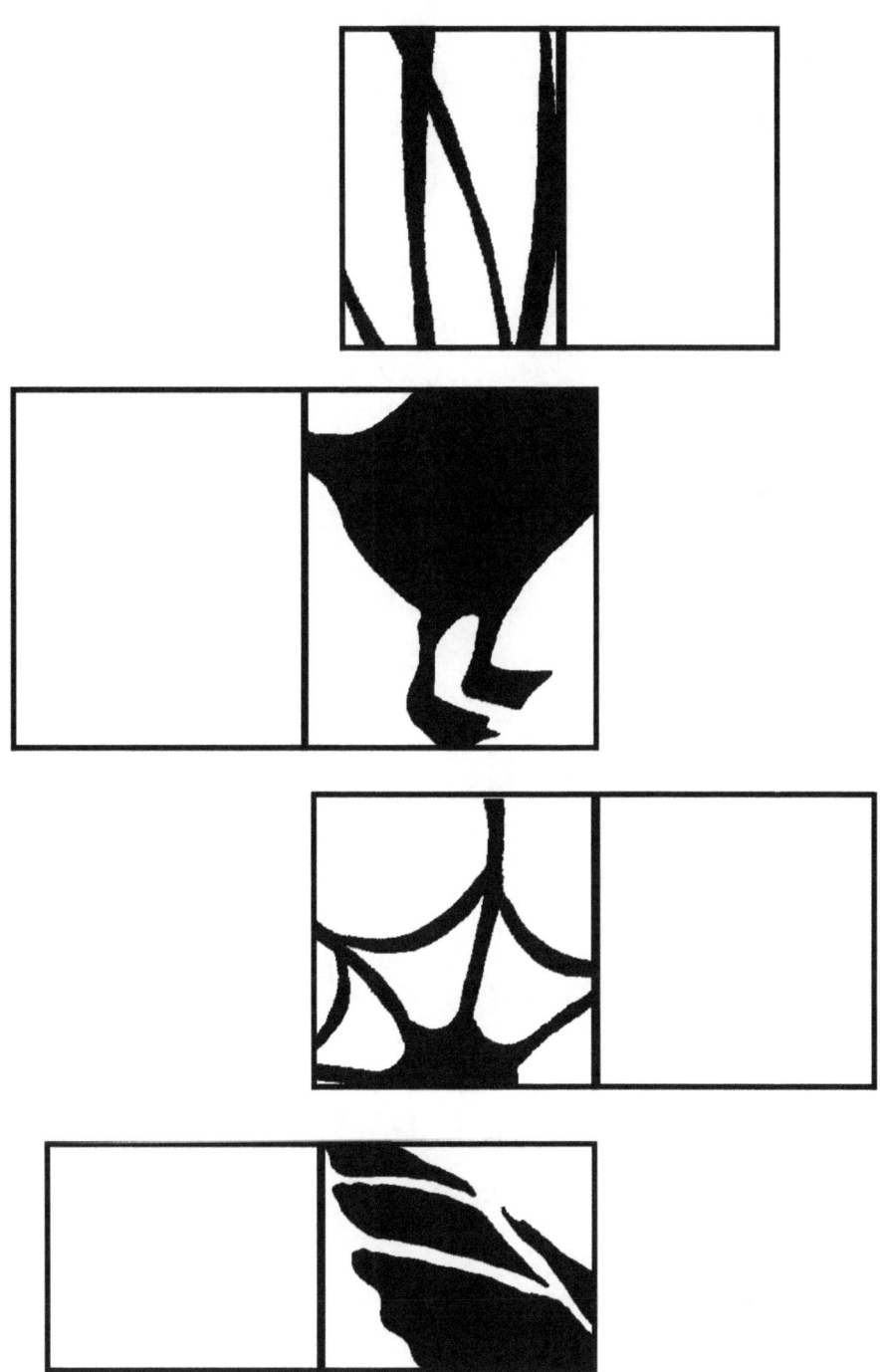

Negative Space • Lesson 10 • Exercise 10-A

Negative Space • Lesson 10 • Exercise 10-B

Negative Space • Lesson 10 • Exercise 10-B

Photo © Stephanie C. Del Bosco

Negative Space • Lesson 10 • Exercise 10-C

89

Loose-leaf sheets for each Exercise are available for printing at www.earthen.com/exercises/

Photo © Stephanie C. Del Bosco

Negative Space • Lesson 10 • Exercise 10-C

Photo © Carolyn Wing Greenlee

Finishing Up

Congratulations on finishing this stage of your artistic adventure! Before you leave this course, please do one more thing.

Revelation Drawings

Please take out five sheets Date each drawing after you've finished it.

1. On sheet #1, draw your favorite subject—whatever you like to draw best.
2. On sheet #2, draw a person from memory.
3. On sheet #3, draw the face below.
4. On sheet #4, draw the chair below.
5. On sheet #5, draw your hand.
6. On the back of each sheet, evaluate your drawings. Use a scale of 1-10, with 10 being the most, and 1 being the least, rate it according to the following state ments:
    A. I like this drawing.
    B. This drawing looks like the model.
    C. I am satisfied with this drawing.
    D. This drawing looks the way I wanted it to.
7. Write your comments about this drawing.

Carolyn's mother, Kathleen Kong Wing when she was about sixteen years old

Thank you. Now go forth and draw with confidence and pleasure, for the Lord has made us in His image, and He is the most creative of all.

From Carolyn Wing Greenlee

When I was little, I loved art. My father made sure I had classes and the best teachers he could find (including master Painter Milford Zornes), but he said art wasn't a very reliable way to make a living and told me I needed to pick something more secure. I always wanted to be a teacher, so I attended Occidental College, graduated in Comparative Literature with an emphasis on poetry, earned my Secondary Credential, and started teaching.

Then came my first tiny, baby boy, John. I chose to be a stay-at-home mom. When John was a few days old, I started taking pictures of him. Then I started taking pictures of the neighborhood kids. Then some of them wanted Senior portraits and then wedding pictures. That's how I became a professional free-lance photographer. Then came baby Thomas.

When John and Thomas were nearly teenagers, I helped start a Christian school and taught art, music, drama, and writing. That's where I met Stephanie. All of them are grown-ups now with wonderful families of their own. I have five grandchildren, some of whom have already graduated from college.

I have had lots of exhibits in galleries and museums—mostly of my photographs—and I've gotten to illustrate books, which was one of my heart's desires, but I'm glad that I listened to my dad because I also became a pretty good writer with fifteen books in print, including the memoirs of my parents and a volume of poetry. In 2004 I was chosen as Poet Laureate of Lake County. I don't know if I would have been as good a writer if I had not been trained in literature.

I was thirty when I decided I wanted to live my life following after Jesus Christ instead of the Taoist-Confucian philosophies my father taught me, which wasn't very satisfying so I tried out a few other religions (such as Hinduism and Zen Buddhism). A lot of people think all religions are basically the same. It's not true. Christianity is totally unique. One of my very favorite parts of that uniqueness is that I can have a deep, rich relationship with the Creator of the Universe, Himself.

I have been a Christian now for more than forty years. It has been an amazing adventure. Living for God has made me more creative, more full, more free, and more alive—not less than I was before.

One time I was telling God how thoughtful He was to put purple flowers on the weeds. "You didn't have to," I said. "You could have made everything gray." He said "I'm so glad you noticed. I made them for hope. Did you ever notice that the first things out of bare branches after winter are not leaves but blossoms? I made them for hope." Here then, is the true heart of God. I pray that as you learn to see with trained and receptive eyes the complexities, varieties, and beauties around you, you will see the true heart of God who makes all His creation a message to you, His beloved child. He, Himself has put desires in your heart. Delight yourself in Him and be surprised at what He brings about.

From Stephanie

I learned to draw when I was eleven with the help of an inspiring teacher who taught me the principles of Right Brain seeing exercises. I took art classes in high school and knew I wanted to major in art in college. In fact, I wanted to go to an art school. My parents said, "Okay, you can be an art major, but you need to get a liberal arts education and you need to major in commercial design or become a teacher of art so you can support yourself financially." My parents were wise and advised me well. I went to a liberal arts school, Pacific Lutheran University, and majored in Graphic Design with a minor in Psychology, thinking I might go into art therapy. If I had it to do again, I would have rather minored in English because writing skills, and even speaking skills, are needed in life more than psychology.

When I was in college, computers were just starting to be used for designing. My strength was in the fine arts, in drawing, and I purposefully didn't take a computer lab class because I did not want to get a job in the city and design at a big company with my desk in a little cubicle, perhaps supporting things I didn't believe it.

After graduating I travelled abroad awhile, then came home and tried to get a job in my hometown. No matter what I did, I couldn't get a job. I kept praying for God's will and direction. Eventually I started working for the inspiring teacher who had taught me to draw when I was eleven. She had a position for me at her publishing company. It is here that I actually used my degree. I learned how to use the computer on the job for designing covers and laying out books. I drew illustrations which used my drawing ability. Also, because it was a publishing company, my writing ability was increased as well. It was a wonderfully supportive place to work, and I learned valuable skills that I still use now.

Later I decided to earn my teaching credential. I was supposed to take a basic computer course, but because of my work at Earthen Vessel, I was able to prove that I could teach a computer class in Graphic Design. They waived the requirement. All of this was because I learned to use the program on the job. This art course was one of the projects I worked on ten years ago when I was just learning how to use the computer for layout and design.

During college, my professor told me that I struggled between two passions: art and people. She said I was a talented artist, but needed to choose because I could not be good at both. I thought that either I would be a good artist living in a flat in a big city, or married with children in a small town, not being an artist at all. I also knew that people, loved ones, would always win over my love of art. Art was always secondary. I prayed for God's will concerning marriage and married my supportive husband Doug. I prayed for God's will concerning children and have three beautiful children, Anna Nicholas, and Luke. I thought marrying meant choosing to not be an artist, but what I found out is Doug actually helped me to be an artist. He has been very supportive of my art, and because he provides financially so well for us, I could buy art supplies, frame my pieces, show and sell artwork. I also can teach on the side, and enjoy teaching small, intimate pastel/drawing classes in the community. Anna and her friends get to enjoy my studio and the art supplies in it as well as the art students that I tutor.

My life experiences have helped me appreciate the significance of this art course that I worked on a decade ago. Since then I have taught many students and have more ideas and skills to use in the creation of *The Art of the Seeing Eye, Part II*.

BIBLIOGRAPHY

Baker, Arthur, *Renaissance Calligraphy.* New York, NY, Dover Publications, Inc., 1981.

Edwards, Betty, *Drawing on the Right Side of the Brain.* Los Angeles, CA, J. P. Tarcher, Inc., 1979.

Graphic Source Clip Art-Printers Dingbats. Wheeling, IL, Graphic Products Corporation, 1989.

Grafton, Carol Belanger, *Ready-To-Use Decorative Letters.* Mineola, NY, Dover Publications, Inc. 1986.

Grafton, Carol Belanger, *Ready-To-Use Old-Fashioned Animal Cuts.* Mineola, NY, Dover Publications, Inc. 1987.

Haeckel, Ernst, *Art Forms in Nature.* New York, NY, Dover Publications, Inc., 1974.

Putnam, William C., *Geology.* New York, Oxford University Press, 1964.

Sandbeck, Ellen, *Ready-To-Use Animal Silhouettes.* Mineola, NY, Dover Publications, Inc. 1989.

Sibbett, Ed Jr., *Bird Cut & Use Stencils.* New York, NY, Dover Publications, Inc., 1981.

Waddell, Roberta, *The Art Nouveau Style.* New York, NY, Dover Publications, Inc., 1977.

Zornes, Milford, *Book of Trees*, Kelseyville, CA, Earthen Vessel Productions, Inc., 2004

Zornes, N.A., Milford, *Milford Zornes in Black & White*, Kelseyvillel, CA, Earthens Vessel Productions, Inc., 2005

www.ingramcontent.com/pod-product-compliance
Lightning Source LLC
LaVergne TN
LVHW061343060426
835512LV00016B/2635